The Avadhoota Whispers of Wisdom

A Young Monk's Didactic Journey Through Nature Unveiling The Profound Wisdom Of Ancient Spiritual Teachings On Self-Discovery

Understanding Hinduism Series – Book 2

Sahasranam Kalpathy

COPYRIGHT

Copyright © 2023 by Sahasranam Kalpathy All rights reserved. No part of this book may be produced or stored in a retrieval system or transmitted in any form by any means, electronic, photocopying, recording, or otherwise, without express written permission of the author.

Disclaimer

All the facts in the books and the statistics given are taken from authentic sources. The suggestions and opinions expressed in the book are the authors own and do not in any way intend to hurt the feelings of anyone or any other religion. Some of the interpretations of the scriptures and texts given in the book may be seem slightly different from the conventional descriptions as it is known that such exegesis can vary depending on the commenting author.

ISBN: 9798859062409

Imprint: Independently published

I pay my sincere homage

to enlightened sages, guiding generations through Hindu philosophy, igniting truth-seekers' motivation across time.

The eternal fire of spirituality fuels passionate hearts pursuing immeasurable wisdom

ACKNOWLEDGEMENTS

I wish to pay my respects to Late Swami Chinmayananda, Swami Udit Chaitanya, and Swami Chidananda Puri for bringing Hinduism and its concepts close to the masses. I was also one who benefitted from their *satsangs*.

My parents and my elderly relatives like uncles and aunts (numerous to be named) have helped me in the spiritual journey in my life. I have to acknowledge their help and guidance with gratitude.

The Swamijis in the Ramakrishna Mission in Kozhikode, Kerala, India have helped me immensely by providing many books on various aspects of Hinduism and spirituality. I humbly bow before all the Swamijis with gratitude.

My family has stood by me during my days of authoring this book and supported me in all manner possible. I will be failing in my duty if I do not acknowledge that.

I must place on record my sincere thanks to Mr. Som Bathla, my mentor in this author journey and all the affectionate members of the Author-Helping-Author (AHA) community who have always given me constructive suggestions at various stages of my writing and publishing.

Some of the contents have been tweaked using Artificial Intelligence software – ChatGPT. I gratefully acknowledge this help.

My thanks are due to Ms. Lolitha *'Revandesigns'* for the beautiful cover designed for this book.

TABLE OF CONTENTS

ACKNOWLEDGEMENTS 4
TABLE OF CONTENTS 5
HERE IS A FREE GIFT FOR YOU 7
PREFACE 9
INTRODUCTION 13
PROLOGUE 17
EARTH 27
AIR 41
SKY 49
WATER 56
FIRE 64
MOON 73
SUN 80
PIGEON 86
PYTHON 94
OCEAN 100
MOTH 108
BEE 113
ELEPHANT 120

DEER	125
FISH	130
PINGALA the COURTESAN	135
HAWK	143
CHILD	147
MAIDEN	152
FLETCHER	158
SERPENT	164
SPIDER	169
WASP	177
EPILOGUE (MY BODY)	182
ANNEXURE	192
RESOURCES & REFERENCES	200
A Humble Request to the Reader	205
ABOUT THE AUTHOR	206
BOOKS BY THE AUTHOR	207

HERE IS A FREE GIFT FOR YOU

Discover The Secrets To A Healthy Heart

Download Your FREE eBook Today!

Did you know that heart disease is the leading cause of health problems worldwide? Don't wait until it's too late — take charge of your heart health today with my **FREE** eBook, "**Diseases of the Heart**."

Coronary Artery Disease: Learn all about it before it's too late. *Heart Failure*: Understand the symptoms and steps for managing this serious condition. *High Blood Pressure*: Discover how to keep your numbers in check and protect your heart. *Atrial Fibrillation*: Find out what causes this common yet dangerous irregular heartbeat.

Click the **LINK** below to download your copy.

Get Your **FREE** eBook Now! **CLICK ON THE LINK BELOW:**

https://sahasranam.ck.page/708a4d8aa7

Or SCAN the QR code below given overleaf

PREFACE

Hinduism has been a baffling and enigmatic religion for the Western world. For the average Hindu who may not be well versed in the *Vedas* or *Upanishads*, it is a way of life that he has been accustomed to from early childhood. For him it is a faith that his parents and spiritual teachers have inculcated in him from the time he was born. For most Hindus, the religion is simple and uncomplicated. He believes in one God or a few Gods and develops a deep devotion towards them. He lives his whole life in intense devotion towards God, not necessarily knowing the great philosophical truths that are expounded in the ancient Hindu scriptures. Because, for him, Hinduism is absolute faith in the God which will give him *Moksha* (salvation). In the bargain, the average Hindu comes to understand various virtues and moral rectitude, which he faithfully follows lest he defy the God whom he deeply reveres.

This book intends to expound a few of the philosophical principles of Hinduism connected with *renunciation* and *detachment*. The is a fictionalization of the story of sage Dattatreya which is described in the eleventh canto of the *Srimad Bhagavatham* written by sage Veda Vyasa. The author has expanded the precepts described briefly in the scripture into a detailed treatise of the doctrines involved, weaving it on to the tapestry of a beautiful story describing the adventure of a young *Brahmachari*[*] who wanders in the world learning these philosophical truths from his experiences in *Nature* and from various creatures he encounters during his journey.

The book is written in simple language so as to bring out the deep philosophical doctrines distinctly. The adventures of sage Dattatreya are described in great detail to make the narrative engaging.

A Glossary has <u>not</u> been included at the end of the book. The *Annexure* appended at the end of the book familiarizes the reader with some of the terms in Hinduism and their significance. These terms have been marked with an Asterisk [*]. Most of the meanings of the Sanskrit words have been underlined in parenthesis to make reading easier without having to resort to a glossary.

At the end of each chapter, a summary has been composed in quatrains to bring out the spirit of the text in a poetic form. This is to add novelty to the text to give the feeling that the sage has recorded the details in Sanskrit verse.

The reader who is interested in the various aspects of Hinduism is referred to the previous book on Hinduism by the author namely, **"Demystifying Hinduism – A Beginner's Guide"** (see **Appendix**) which is the first book in this series of *'Understanding Hinduism'*. Most of the Sanskrit words and phrases used in this book have been elaborated in the previous book and hence will help the reader get a better insight into the various aspects of Hinduism.

Although the story mainly follows a sannyasi, the text also contains practical advice for regular people on how to lead a happy and fulfilled life, stemming from its underlying philosophical ideas. Some of these philosophical concepts appear in different chapters more than once. This repetition aims to highlight their importance and how they relate to the chapter's content.

Initially, the book delineates the approaches one ought to embrace when delving into the exploration of any subject. This elucidation is conveyed by the *Guru* to their *Sishya*, accompanied by illustrative instances showcasing the methodologies for drawing conclusions through meticulous observation. Furthermore, the *Guru* imparts guidance to the student regarding the virtues intrinsic to a disciple, shedding light on the process of shaping one's character in alignment with these ideals.

A detailed list of *Resources and Bibliography* has been included at the end for the benefit of the reader who may be interested in knowing more about the Hindu way of life.

This is a book both for adults and children. the book mainly targets the youth of today and the Hindu diaspora abroad, so that they get a better understanding about Hinduism. Thus, many of the misconceptions and fallacies about the religion can be cleared in their minds.

With these simple words, I humbly submit this book to my dear readers.

Sahasranam Kalpathy.

(Dr. K. V. Sahasranam)

ramani2911@gmail.com

INTRODUCTION

Hinduism, better known as '*Sanatana Dharma*,' is the most ancient religion in the world. Unlike most religions, Hinduism is a religion with many scriptures and texts. Hindus do not follow any single text. Of the numerous such texts in Hinduism, *Srimad Bhagavatham* also called the *Bhagavata Purana* is one of the preeminent texts. It was written by Veda Vyasa who had already codified the *Shruthis** (that which is heard) into the four *Vedas** namely, *Rig, Yajur, Sama* and the *Atharva Vedas*. After having written the eighteen *Puranas**, sage Veda Vyasa was still feeling discontented and felt that something worthwhile was lacking from his compositions. It was then that the celestial sage *Narada** met him and advised him to write about the Absolute Supreme Godhead, the *Brahman*. The sage advised him to write about *Bhagavan Narayana* (Vishnu) and bring out his virtues, Avatars and show the way to *Moksha** (salvation). Thus, was born the *Srimad Bhagavatam*. The whole Purana has been written in the form of a dialogue between the Sage Suka, son of Sage Vyasa and the King Parikshit.

King Parikshit was the son of Abhimanyu, son of Arjuna the third of the Pandavas. He succeeded King Yudhishtra to the throne.

Once, king Parikshit was hunting in the forest when he was separated from his entourage . As he felt thirsty, he approached an *Ashramam* which he saw in the forest. Sage Shamika was in deep meditation in the *Ashramam* and did not notice the king. The king, out of sudden anger and arrogance picked up the carcass of a dead snake he found nearby and put it on the sage's neck and left in a huff. The sage's son Shringi who returned to the hermitage found his father with a dead snake around his neck and was enraged. He cursed that whoever did this shall die on the seventh day bitten by *Takshaka*, the king of serpents. The king regretted his rash act when he came to know of the sage's curse.

King Parikshit gave up his throne to his son Janamejaya and sat in penance for seven days. During this period, the *Srimad Bhagavatham* was explained in detail to him by Sage Suka who was the son of sage Vyasa.

It is a voluminous text which is divided into 12 cantos with 335 chapters and 18,000 verses. It discusses the various *Avatars** of *Bhagavan Vishnu* and recounts the story of *Sri Krishna* in great detail. The *Bhagavata Purana*, among other things, also discusses Cosmology, Astronomy, Genealogy, Geography, Music, Dance, Yoga and Culture. *Advaita**, where the Supreme Godhead is described as a single Omnipotent, Omniscient and Omnipresent entity, is exhaustively illustrated in the *Srimad Bhagavatham*. This monism is the crux of the text. *Bhakti* (devotion) leads to *Moksha* (salvation) and bliss. The *Srimad Bhagavatham* contains the quintessence of all the *Vedas* and *Vedantic* literature.

The eleventh canto of the Srimad Bhagavatam contains the story of an *Avadhoota** who is also called sage *Dattatreya*. Before his ascent to the heavens, *Bhagavan Sri Krishna* advised his companion and confidante, Uddhava on the various aspects of *Dharma** and *Bhakti*, and he described the story of King Yadu. Once the king met a mendicant who seemed carefree, very happy and blissful. The mendicant was *Dattatreya*, an *Avadhoota*. The king enquired as to how he could be so happy and pleasant in the midst of all the trials and tribulations in the world around him. The mendicant who had realized the *Brahman* and hence was free of all worldly concerns explained to the king about his twenty-four '*Gurus*'* who taught him all that he knew. This '*Yadu-Avadhoota Samvadam*'* (discussion) forms the basis of this book. The whole discussion which is described in the eleventh canto in chapters 7 – 9 forms the basis of this fictionalization.

Dattatreya was the son of sage Atri and wife Anasuya. Having acquired the spiritual knowledge from his mentor and father Sage Atri and having become an *Avadhoota*, *Dattatreya* met King Yadu who asked him how he was able to spend a cheerful life free of attachment. The *Avadhoota* then described the various *Gurus* he encountered during his jaunts through the countryside learning from animate and inanimate creations in the world. He described what he learnt using his power of **Observation**.

The book is written as memoirs of Datta who, on the advice of his Guru, leaves the comfort of his *Ashramam** and goes in search of knowledge from *Nature* and the wide world. He encounters many creatures and gains knowledge from them. He understands the secret of **Selfless Service** and **Detachment** from the five elements - the Earth, Water, Air, Space, and Fire. He even figures out the truth about **Renunciation** and **Realization of the Supreme Godhead** from a prostitute. Thus, the wanderings of the sage lead him through many experiences which teach him the truth about life and how to achieve contentment and happiness while living in this material world.

In essence, the journey of the sage *Dattatreya*, in search of knowledge can be summarized in the words of Rudyard Kipling who described the six methods of acquiring knowledge:

> *I keep six honest serving-men*
> *(They taught me all I knew);*
> *Their names are What and Why and When*
> *And How and Where and Who.*
>
> *I send them over land and sea,*
> *I send them east and west;*
> *But after they have worked for me,*
> *I give them all a rest.*

PROLOGUE

The Guru was sitting on a mat in deep meditation. He was attired in ochre clothes and his greying beard and twisted locks of silvery hair on the top of his head gave him a majestic look. His eyes were closed and he was sitting erect. An oil lamp glowed in a corner of his cottage with its effulgent flame dispelling the darkness. It was early morning before sunrise, the *Brahma muhurtam** when it is said that Goddess *Saraswathi*, the Goddess of Knowledge goes around the world blessing whoever is indulging in *Vedic* practices during this auspicious time of the day. The whole world was silent. Even the animals in his ashram, the cows, the goats, and the deer were in slumber. The birds in the trees around this hermitage had not yet stirred into action with their shrill calls. The pall of darkness around the ashram gave the whole atmosphere an eerie feel.

Close by him stood Datta, his son and *shishya* (disciple). He was a tall handsome youth with sharp intelligent eyes and an aquiline nose that gave his countenance a dignified look. He was fair in complexion and wore the ochre clothes of a monk. His dark black hair was tied into a bun at the top of his head and his trim beard added to his august personality. He stood with folded hands waiting for his father and *Guru* to complete his meditation. As he stood there, his lips were chanting the *Gayatri mantra** and his mind was focused on the task ahead.

Datta had completed part of his education and training under his father's tutelage and was waiting for his father's orders for the next phase of his education. Sage Atri had taught him the *Vedas**, the *Upanishads** and all the *Puranas** in addition to the *Vedangas** and the essentials of the *Sanatana Dharma* (Eternal Religion) which every *sishya* had to learn. He had understood the recondite principles of the scriptures in *Santana Dharma* and had assimilated all the knowledge in the last nine years when he had been formally inducted into his father's *Gurukulam**. His *Upanayanam** ceremony when he donned the *Poonal* (sacred thread) heralded his entry into the stage of the *Brahmachari** from his childhood. The *Upanayanam* ceremony gave him the status of a *Dvija** (twice born) and endowed him with the responsibility of learning the scriptures in his religion. In the last nine years he had completed the learning of the scriptures and now awaited the next stage of his education. The Sage Atri was to announce it today.

Datta had been nine years old when his *Upanayanam* ceremony was conducted and now he was a strapping youth of eighteen. He had learnt to control his senses and desires and knew the art of meditation and all the *Ashtanga Yogas**. His daily *Hatha Yoga** exercises had transformed him into a muscular lad with chiseled features and radiant countenance, which made him attractive and handsome. His tall stature added to his personality.

Datta stood with folded hands and bowed head in front of his father waiting for his father to complete his meditation and reveal the details of the next phase of his training.

Sage Atri opened his eyes and he saw his son standing in a corner of his hermitage. A gentle smile spread across his lips.

"Datta, I am pleased with your training thus far," he said in a deep voice, "Now it is time to commence the next phase of your education".

"Yes, Guru", Datta replied humbly. "I wait for your advice."

"The next phase of your indoctrination will be practical training where you teach yourself using your power of **observation** and **deduction**. Before going into the details of it, I will give you a short account of how you teach yourself to arrive at logical and practical conclusions. Listen."

The sage went on, "There are six principles involved in acquiring knowledge from this world. These are called '*Pramanas**' (proofs, learning technique). These are the means to acquire authentic knowledge about the world. You will understand them better when I elaborate upon them. The basic three elements of learning are to know ***why*** *you have to learn something,* ***what*** *you need to learn* and ***how*** *to learn it.* Initially, I will reveal to you ***how*** to acquire this knowledge. This will help you in your further pursuit of knowledge."

- The first is **Pratyaksha Pramana** which means learning from one's own first-hand experience. You know that fire can burn anything. A child learns this when he puts his finger to a flame. This is the learning involving your sense organs. The sense organs contribute to learning by involving your emotion.
- **Anumana Pramana** is the second one. Here you learn from questioning and arrive at conclusions based on logical reasoning or inference. You derive your answers logically by reflecting. Why does a rose bush have thorns? You logically conclude that it is to deter pests from attacking the plant.
- When you learn from examples and analogies, it is called **Upamana Pramana**. For example, you know that the earth is spherical in shape as has been described in the *Srimad Bhagavatham*. The earth has been described as a *Bhoogolam* (globe). This is derived from the example of all the other heavenly bodies like the sun, moon and the planets which are also heavenly bodies and hence spherical in shape. So, you conclude that the earth, being a heavenly body, would also be round and ball shaped. You have not seen a wild bison. But if I say that it almost looks like a buffalo, you will get an idea of how a bison will look like. This is an example of Upamana Pramana.
- **Arthapatti Pramana** is the method by which you extrapolate a fact to learn and presume certain other facts. It is postulation or derivation from circumstances. From one fact, you should derive more facts. An example would be if you see smoke at a distance, you presume that there should be a fire there. If you see dark clouds on the horizon, you presume that it will rain in a short while.

- When you learn from a *negative conclusion* or a non-perception, you call it **Anupalabdi Pramana**. It is as if you are deriving a fact from what is not there. It is a negative proof of what is not there or what you are **not** seeing. It is the perception of the non-existence of a thing. You cannot perceive it by the senses. When you see an empty classroom, you decide that the students are absent from the class that day. Perhaps it is a holiday. When you see a glass half full of water, you presume that the other half is empty.
- The last one is the **Sabda Pramana** which is learning from the spoken word and the testimony from the experts and scholars. What you learn from your *Gurus* or what you read from the scriptures and texts is the *Sabda Pramana*. Whatever you have learnt from me is all *Sabda Pramana*."

The sage continued, "Thus, you find, my dear boy, that it is **inquisitiveness** that leads you to effective learning. Questioning things leads you to acquire knowledge. This teaches you as to **how** to learn things. When you apply these self-teaching skills and use **Prayoga** (experiments) in your learning process, your knowledge will become complete. But know that the greatest path to knowledge is to develop your power of **Observation** and **Logical Deduction**."

Datta bowed his head in reverence, "I understand this O! great Guru. Your benevolence in teaching me has consummated my scriptural knowledge and transformed me. Now please command me as to what I should do to further my knowledge of the world and attain self-realization and attain a stage of spiritual consciousness beyond worldly concern and become an *Avadhoota*."

Sage Atri smiled, "Datta, you have learnt the theory part of all the scriptures. But you should understand that education is not complete by learning from the Guru only. Haven't you heard the *sloka* (verse)."

आचार्यात् पादमादत्ते, पादं शिष्यः स्वमेधया ।
सब्रह्मचारिभ्यः पादं, पादं कालक्रमेण च ॥

Acharyat padamadatte,

Padam shishyah swamedhaya |

Sa-Brahmacharibhyah Padam,

padam kalakramena cha ||

One fourth from the teacher,

One fourth from own intelligence

One fourth from classmates,

And one fourth only with time.

"One-fourth of your knowledge comes from your *Guru* (teacher). This indicates that a good teacher will help and guide you to proper knowledge. But if a student does not learn his scriptures and lessons, the fault lies not with the *Guru* alone. It also depends on the attitude and the earnestness of the student. The Guru's main aim in teaching is to kindle the fire of knowledge in the mind of the student. The student should be able to further his knowledge by his own efforts aided by curiosity and interest. The teacher can only guide the student as to how to learn."

"Another one-fourth of the knowledge is acquired by the student himself depending on his ability, aptitude, and intelligence. The student must learn by himself. To cure a disease, a patient must take the medicine himself as no one else can help him. The doctor can only prescribe the medicine. Similarly, the student, by his untiring efforts and self-study should endeavor to acquire one-fourth of the knowledge himself."

"Another one-fourth of the knowledge of a student is derived from his peers and classmates. This is acquired by group study, discussions, and debates with his fellow students. Such deliberations with his peers advances his knowledge in course of time."

"The final one-fourth of the student's knowledge is attained in the course of time from personal experience in the wide world. *Experience converts the theoretical aspects of your knowledge into practical wisdom*. What you have learnt from me, from the scriptures and from your friends and peers should be put to practical use in the world and there is a lot that you will learn from the world around you. This practical experience comes over time from life itself. **The worst part of ignorance is to be ignorant of one's own ignorance.** No amount of academic teaching or learning can substitute for practical experience."

"You have learnt everything that I taught you. Similarly, you have learnt a lot by discussions, debates, and deliberations from your friends. You have put in hours of study to learn many of the lessons yourself. So now, what remains for you is to learn from practical experience."

"A true student should have the following characteristics:

काकदृष्टि बकध्यानम्, श्वाननिरद्रा तथैव च ।

अल्पाहारं जीर्णवस्त्रम्, एतत् विद्यार्थि लक्षणम् ।।

Kaaka Drishti Bhagadhyanam,
Svana nidra thathaiva cha
Alpahaaram Jeerna vastram,
Ethath Vidhyarthi Lakshanam

The power of keen observation like a crow, concentration like a stork, being alert even in sleep like a dog, eating little food and wearing simple clothes. These are the qualities that students should have.

Datta humbly bowed before his *Guru* and father, "Pray, tell me what I should do now to acquire the one-fourth knowledge that I lack and have to learn. How do I go about achieving that?"

"Yes, my son, the Guru intoned, "I have kept ready your effects in that corner. There is a bundle of palm leaves with a couple of styluses for you to write with. Record your observations and conclusions in it. Your *Kamandalu* (water pot) is there. Your clothes and other essentials are in that corner. And there is a *danda* (staff) in the corner. It will help you climb steep hills and mountains. Take these and commence your journey in life."

"During the next four months" continued the sage, "You shall go around the country and learn your lessons from *Nature* and the wide world. There is a lot to learn from observing *Nature*. Start with the *Panchabhootas* (five elements). The *Earth, Water, Fire, Sky* and *Air*

Palm Leaf Scripts

are the five primary elements in Nature and you will learn a lot from them. Begin by observing them and reflecting on what they can teach you."

"Then, there are your five senses of *Touch, Hearing, Vision, Smell* and *Taste*. You will learn a lot from these. Observe very carefully whatever you see all around you during your journey and record your observations and inferences during these four months. You will realize by **contemplation** and **reflection** what *Nature* has to teach you. You will also learn from people and places you see on the way. Derive knowledge from all sources that you come across. At the end of your journey, your wisdom and knowledge will improve manyfold, and you will be much richer and proficient. That is the last stage of your education where you learn using your keen sense of *observation* and *deduction*. This experience will prove very valuable to you in your pilgrimage to become an *Avadhoota*."

Datta prostrated before his Guru and father and went inside the *Ashram* to bid good bye to his mother Anasuya and seek her blessings before undertaking the expedition. She was busy preparing for an induction ritual of the new *Sishyas* (disciples) who would be joining the *Ashram* that day. Datta prostrated before his mother and told her that he would be away for the next four months seeking knowledge from *Nature*.

"*Vijayee Bhava*" (may you be victorious) "*Ayushman Bhava*" (may you have a long life) said his mother blessing him placing her palms on his head. May you return victorious in your ventures and bring glory to the *Santana Dharma*.

Thus began Datta's journey into the wide world and wilderness of Nature in pursuit of self-realization and eternal knowledge hoping that he would be transformed into an *Avadhoota* when his enlightenment was complete.

EARTH

Datta commenced his journey and left his hermitage carrying his bundle of belongings, his *Kamandalu* and his *danda*. His feet were protected by his wooden *Padukas* (wooden footwear). He walked briskly till he reached the outskirts of the village where his father's *Ashram* (hermitage) stood. He decided to begin studying the *Panchabhootas* first.

The **Bhoomi** or **Prithvi** (earth) was the first and most important of them. He decided to start with the earth first and analyze what he could learn from it. At the outskirts of the village, the vast plains stretched in front of him and at a distance he discerned the dark blue mountains silhouetted against the blue sky. Datta entered the plains and began walking forward and observing what he saw. The sun guided the direction of his travel.

Large stretches of paddy fields lay in front of him. Farmers were busy ploughing the fields preparing the soil for the next crop. The ploughs were drawn by oxen harnessed to them. The earth was been furrowed by the ploughs. Datta saw a group of laborers digging a deep well to seek water for the paddy fields. Some women were resting in the shade of a large banyan tree that stood majestically at the corner of the field spreading its branches and casting abundant shade for man and animals to rest. Two ends of a rope hung looped from one of the branches of a tree. To the ends of it was tied a woman's *sari** in the form of a sling in which lay an infant. The mother was gently swinging the sling, singing a soothing lullaby praising the childhood exploits of Sri Krishna. A few cows were grazing in a field nearby. Men were busy in the paddy fields, some manuring the fields and others planting paddy seedlings in the already ploughed and manured field.

Datta saw the contrasts on the surface of the earth. Here was a plain ground with fields and pastures where people cultivated grains, vegetables and tubers which provided their principal food. The pastures provided fodder for the grazing animals like cows and goats. But far away he could see the dark outline of the mountains which were dense with fauna and flora of the earth. The mountains were covered with forests and trees which stood tall against the sky.

Datta walked slowly across the plains and reached the foot of the mountain that he had seen from afar. Looking up, he saw that the mountain stood majestically in front of him dark, silent, and covered with trees and shrubs. The forest was dense. He had to cross the forest to travel beyond the mountain. He was sure that the mountain was home to wild animals and various other creatures in addition to the tall trees whose tops were almost embracing the clouds.

Datta looked at the sun which was approaching the horizon and he realized that sunset was perhaps an hour or two away. He decided to rest for the day and pursue his journey the next morning. Datta found a stream of crystal clear water flowing down from the top of the mountain and beside the stream he found a large sprawling mango tree casting a wide shade all around. He decided to spend the night under the tree.

The water in the stream was cool and refreshing. He drank the cool water and ate the food that his mother had packed for him in a banana leaf. He knew very well that this was his last homely meal and hereafter he would have to rely on edible fruits and berries from the trees and plants on the way or depend on alms that he would receive from the houses in the villages which he would pass through. Datta placed the bundle of possessions under his head and lay down in the cool shade of the tree. He began contemplating on all that he had observed on his journey here. He would derive conclusions from his observations and the next day he would write them down in the palm leaf scripts using the metal stylus provided by his *Guru*. In his mind, he began to recollect the observations of the day.

He heard a rustling noise beside him and he turned his head to see a strikingly beautiful maiden standing in front of him. She was clad in a forest green robe that seemed to billow all around her. Her hair was adorned with fragrant flowers and there was a heavenly charm about her.

Datta stood up flabbergasted, "Who are you, young maiden? And what are you doing in this forest?"

The maiden smiled, "I am **Bhoomi Devi,** *Goddess of the Earth.* You seem to have a lot to learn about me and my domain. I know what you have in mind. The earth is my domain and all changes on earth are done by me.

Datta bowed before her and said, "During my travels here, I noticed that man causes much damage and devastation to the earth. He digs, ploughs, and defiles the earth in innumerable ways. But you bear it with tolerance and patience. I was wondering about it."

"Yes, listen to me", said Bhoomi Devi, "I will tell you all about me and my realm and you will learn a lot from it."

* * *

"I have been blessed with a unique characteristic of **Tolerance**, **Forgiveness** *and* **Patience**. *I have been known to be steadfast in my regular Dharma* whatever harm happens around me. People defile me in all ways as you saw, they tear apart my body with the plough, they dig into my system and pollute my body with all sorts of stuff including corpses and toxic waste. But I tolerate all of these and do not retaliate in any way."*

"People abrade my surface for various reasons. They hammer at me with heavy mallets to break the rocks and stones on my face to use them to construct homes for themselves. Man digs, trenches and bores into my bowels to remove precious metals like gold and gems like diamonds and emeralds. It is painful for me but I still bear it with fortitude and give up my precious possessions to man without any hesitation or protest."

"I provide sanctuary to all the rivers of the earth, the trees, the animals the birds and every creature that God created. Some live on my surface whereas some of the birds and other tiny creatures are supported by the trees which

cover my surface. Still others burrow into my bosom creating long ramifying tunnels within my body and live there. I support all of them without any grievance. I forgive all the hurt that man and other creatures inflict on me."

"The trees and plants are my best companions. They clothe me with their greenery and give me all the nourishment I need, and in the bargain they nourish themselves. The trees which I nurture and grow provide fruit to the animals and man. The leaves of the plants and trees are food for the herbivores. The trees also follow my lead and provide selfless service to man and other creatures. When laden with fruit, the trees bow down low so that small animals too may avail themselves of their fruit and leaves. Large trees that adorn the earth are home to a variety of birds, insects and small creatures like squirrels and simians. And the trees never demand anything in return. Where else can you see this type of selfless sacrifice? This is how wise men are. They act in the world without expecting others to recompense for their kindness."

"The tree teaches you not to be attached to material possessions or regret their loss. When fruits ripen, the trees relinquish their attachment to the fruits and let them drop to the ground. It never holds on to the fruit of its actions like man. Even in death, the tree follows selfless Karma*. The birds pick up the twigs from the fallen tree to build their nest. The tree gives up its trunk and branches to construct homes for man. And to warm himself and prepare his food, man burns the wood from the fallen trees. Nay, all is not over. Even the ashes from the burnt wood provide nourishment to other trees and plants on earth and thus this cycle of altruistic service goes on. Does man do anything like this? The wise among men, the Sattvic*, the sages and ascetics do practice such selfless service knowing fully well that it is the only way to self-realization and Moksha (salvation)."

"The tree in spring and summer is fully covered with rich foliage of leaves which helps in nourishing the tree and providing it energy and life. But come fall, the leaves become aged, change color and fall. But the tree does not mourn the dead and fallen leaves. The fallen leaves in turn provide a carpet at the foot of the tree and over time turn into manure and nourish the same tree. The tree never holds on to its valuable possession, the leaves, but let go without remorse. But man does not learn from this. He holds tight to his material possessions and does not let go of them even at the time of death knowing fully well that he would have no use for it after death. Man should take a leaf out of the tree's life to learn to 'let go' when the time comes. A wise man learns to use the failures in life as manure for his growth like the fallen leaves and learns **detachment** from the trees."

"Look at my mountains. They raise their majestic heads far above the clouds, but their feet are firmly rooted on the earth. Man should endeavor to be like them. However

tall or great he is he must be humble and have his feet firmly rooted to the ground. Arrogance and haughtiness should not overpower him and cloud his intellect. Man should learn this **humility** from the mountains which bedeck my body like my breasts. The mountains provide habitats for all types of creatures from large predators to tiny reptiles and insects. All these creatures live in harmony with mutual cooperation in the mountains balancing the eco system. The only creature which defies all this is man. He takes undue advantage of the forests, the wealth of resources in the mountains and the rivers. Man takes more than he needs and deserves. He takes more due to his greed than for his need. A predator will kill only to eat. It never kills for pleasure or out of anger and spite. But man, in his ignorance and arrogance kills each other in the name of land, wealth and possessions. He also kills for lust and greed. Man should learn the technique of contentment from the animals in the forest. He should learn the need for interdependence and collaboration from other living creatures."

"And look at me. I never waver from my duty whatever harm comes to me or my possessions. I keep steadfast in my path of Dharma*. I go around the Sun daily with a fixed schedule brought on by unwavering discipline and never for a moment digress from this path of action which has been assigned to me. Humans should learn these traits of **discipline** and **duty** from me".

"In my world, seasons change. The pleasant spring leads to a scorching summer which is followed by windy autumn and then a harsh winter. But I bear all this with equal tolerance. Heavy rains may pelt the mountains leading to landslides and rockfalls. A heavy winter may create avalanches in the mountains. But the mountains are least affected by all these. The mountains and the plains bear all this with composure."

"Similarly, man should learn to adapt to the harsh circumstances and vicissitudes of life and not get unnerved by it. When winter comes, one should realize that spring is not far behind. Once man learns to adapt to circumstances and accept the joys and sorrows of life with aplomb, he will learn to be a Sthithaprajna*. If so, the vagaries of life will not affect his mind and disturb it."

"Similarly, you can see beautiful flowers like the rose in my earth's garden. But the rose bush is often filled with thorns. This is to protect it from insects and other creatures which tend to destroy the flower. But you would never hate the rose as its plant has thorns. No, why because you accept the rose with its thorns and all. Similarly, the wise man learns to accept others with their faults and goodness. You cannot separate goodness and faults in a person and like him or hate him for it."

"Look at the creatures in the garden of Nature. You can see the ant squirreling away food for the future, for the winter when it cannot scout around for morsels of food. The honey bee gathers nectar and stores it in its hive for future use. But neither the ant nor the bee anguish over the future and spend anxious moments worrying about the future. Man is the only 'animal' that feels anxious for the future and fails to live in the present. All other creatures on earth live for the present hardly worrying about what will happen in future."

"Look at the herd of deer grazing at the edge of the forest. They are playfully prancing about oblivious of the menacing danger in the forest in the form of a vicious predator. The deer is not anxious of what will happen to it if and when the predator attacks. It resorts to the fight or flight response at the sight of danger. But unlike man, the deer does not waste time mulling anxiously over the future. Likewise, a wise man and a saint never think anxiously of the future but live in the joyous present."

"On the earth you find plants and trees grown by man for his benefit like the plants that give him vegetables for food and trees that yield sweet fruit. But the farmer takes pains to cultivate these beneficial plants which provide him with food by taking care of them nurturing them, watering them, and manuring the soil. But the weeds that grow in between these plants do so without any effort on the part of man. They grow faster, copious and abundant compared to the cultivated plants."

"Good and evil are like this. Humans do not realize this. Goodness in man is like the cultivated plants. One needs to nurture and painfully pursue positive and good habits to cultivate them whereas evil spreads in him like weeds, effortlessly and readily. Nature is not partial to either the useful plants or the weeds. If man is careless, the weeds of evil grow within him unchecked."

"On earth, various animals have various skills. A cuckoo can sing beautifully. But a peacock can dance beautifully. A swan gives you delight but moves alone. But the stork knows community living. A horse can run very fast. But monkeys can climb trees easily. A fish swims efficiently in water, but a squirrel scurries up the tree very briskly but would drown in water. Thus, each creature is endowed with a different skill, and it is happy and satisfied with what it possesses. Man alone is an exception to this. He is always jealous or envious of the skills of other humans and does not pay attention to what skills or talents he possesses. Life will always be an eternal conflict of interests for such a person. The wise man, however, learns to recognize the skills and talents that he has and take advantage of them."

"Let me tell you a simple story. Once there was a small mango seedling which sprouted out of a seed that was dropped on the wayside by a bird which had fed on a ripe mango. The seed sprouted into a small plant. Recognizing the plant, the villagers watered it and manured the soil around the plant. They took care of the plant and put up a fence around it to prevent the grazing animals from getting at its leaves. A few years went by, and the plant became a large mango tree and one season, it blossomed and had plenty of luscious fruits – mangoes - dangling from its branches. The very same villagers who had carefully nurtured the tree hitherto, started pelting stones at the tree, for they wanted to get at the mangoes that were hanging from the tree. Man is like that. Whenever he finds a person who is successful, he 'pelts stones' at them because human nature is one of jealousy and spite."

"But the mango tree is more Dharmic* than man. Whenever someone pelted a stone at the tree, the tree would, as a return gesture, provide him with a luscious ripe mango. Man should learn from the tree to do good even to those who harm you. Wise men and saints are like that. They do good even to those who harm them. Learn this life's secret from the mango tree in my earth's garden."

"Man is always in a hurry. But I never hurry. Hurrying is not an attribute of Nature, but in course of time I get everything accomplished. I have my own rhythm and pace while performing my manifold tasks. Be it the growing of a tree or flourishing of a forest, everything in its own time – is my dictum. Never hurry, for hurry can lead to worry. Man should learn this from Nature. Another great lesson the wise should learn from me is that the two things **Flexibility** and **Adaptability** are my two great characteristics. If man learns of these two facets of my nature, he would be immensely successful in life."

"I wish man realizes that men may come, and men may die, but I go on forever. This earth of mine is here for *generations to come. Man must realize this and not resort to wanton destruction and desecration of my ecological system. For I have to sustain for generations to come and man should endeavor to preserve Nature and not defile it. He should remember that the earth is a legacy that he has to leave for generations to come."*

Bhoomi Devi looked at Datta with an enigmatic smile. *"I hope you have assimilated whatever knowledge I wanted you to get out of me. The good earth is silently revolving around its axis day after day, year after year and for eons without ever digressing from its bounden duty. Try to be like the earth and its flora and fauna which teach you all these hidden secrets."*

* * *

Datta awoke suddenly realizing that he had been asleep. The sun had already risen. The previous night's episode flashed through his mind. He was not sure if what he had seen, heard and experienced was a dream or reality. The detailed conversation with *Bhoomi Devi* was lingering in his mind. He decided to commit it to writing and picked up his bundle of palm leaves and the stylus. For the next one hour he remained engrossed in writing down his observations and inferences of the previous day.

It was the beginning of a new day, and the sun was peeping out from between the leaves of the tree and the birds were stirring filling the atmosphere with their sweet melodies. Datta went to the stream, bathed, and spent some time in *Japa** and meditation and decided to go on his way to face another bright day of adventure. On the way he would find fruit from the trees in the forest which would give him food for nourishment.

Datta realized that the Earth taught him the importance of **Patience, Tolerance** and **Forgiveness**. **Discipline** and **Duty** were the other attributes he learned from the Earth. The trees taught him **Detachment** and **Selfless** Service. The mountains showed him the importance of **Humility** and the creatures taught him **Co-operative endeavor**. **Flexibility** and **Adaptability** were two other important lessons that he learnt from Nature.

He shouldered his bundle, picked up his *danda* and *Kamandalu* and began his journey for the day.

* * *

Datta's Observations – Summary

EARTH

From Mother Earth, learn tolerance's art,
A balm for wounds, a salve for every heart.
With forgiving eyes, she heals the land,
Her boundless love, like oceans, grand.

The mountains tall, in humbleness stand,
Teaching us to bow, and to understand,
That greatness lies not in prideful mirth,
But in the gentleness that marks our worth.

Cooperation's song, from creatures all,
In harmony, they heed the *Nature's* call.
From the smallest ant to the mighty beast,
United spirits, the greatest feast.

Embrace the changing seasons' sway,
Tolerance blooms like flowers in May.
With every shift, a chance to grow,
In winds of change, wisdom's seeds sow.

Contentment's wisdom, birds softly sing,
Their cheerful melodies, blessings they bring.
And animals, in tranquil repose,
Lead us the path that inner peace shows.

Living joyfully in the present's embrace,
A precious gift, a fleeting grace.
Like cattle grazing, worries abate,
In life's unfolding, be present, not late.

The mango tree with fruits so sweet,
Teaches kindness when others mistreat.
Returning good for every harm,
A healing gesture, a soothing balm.

Detachment, from the trees we find,
Let possessions not cloud the mind.
Free as leaves that gently roam,
Find solace in being, not having a home.

Nature whispers truth, in whispers,
She calls Adaptability, the key that enthralls.
In flexibility strength is found,
To weather life's storms, to stand firm on the ground.

So let us learn from Nature's grace,
In every challenge, find our place.
With open hearts and minds, we'll see,
The wisdom gifted by Earth's decree.

AIR

Datta decided to climb the mountain. Looking up, he found the mountain tall and menacing. This would take almost a day as he found the mountain very steep and seemingly impossible to climb. But he knew from his father's teaching that *the journey of a thousand miles always starts with a single step.* Yes, one step at a time would be how he would conquer this mountain and ascend it. With this firm resolve, he slowly shuffled forward using his *danda* for support. The next two hours found him halfway up to the top of the mountain. The foliage around him was becoming dense and the forest was getting thicker. It was then that he heard a faint whooshing sound like running water. He moved towards the sound and found himself in a clearing in the forest. Before him he found a large waterfall almost fifty feet high. It created a whirling pool at the bottom. Datta decided to rest here for a while and sat on a rock near the waterfall.

He felt the cool breeze envelop him and swathe him with droplets of water refreshing to the body, mind, and soul. A strange sense of peace engulfed him in this serene surroundings. After resting awhile, he decided to look around the clearing. A mango tree stood nearby laden with fresh, ripe, luscious fruits. He collected a few fruits for himself and drank the cool water from the pool. He filled his *Kamandalu* with fresh water. The sweet smell of jasmine flowers carried by the gentle breeze that swirled around him assailed his olfactory senses. Soon he found that the scent of the jasmine mingled with another scent stronger and more aromatic. It was from a tree that had blossomed and was covered with a crown of white flowers. Some of the flowers had been shed from the tree forming a white carpet beneath the tree. The scent was overpowering to the senses. It gave him a strange sense of peace.

Datta decided to push on and reach the summit of the mountain where he could rest and take a break. It was noon and the sun was blazing overhead, and he felt tired. He decided to find an appropriate place to rest till evening. At a distance he saw a group of trees surrounded by a pleasing and inviting verdure. He walked towards the copse of trees to rest beneath its soothing shade. He sat on a rock under the tree, leaned against the tree trunk and drank a mouthful of water from his *Kamandalu*.

The soothing westerly cool breeze that wafted through the branches of the trees carrying the mixed sweet aroma of the flowers gently tickled his body. Datta closed his eyes.

He felt a gentle hand shaking his shoulder. Datta opened his eyes to see an almost transparent human form in front of him. He was clad in a diaphanous robe which seemed to swirl around him in waves. He was a strikingly handsome young man with sparkling eyes and a cherubic face. His limbs moved in a rhythmic undulating movement as he spoke, "Who are you and why are you sitting here in the middle of nowhere in this mountain?"

"I am Datta, the son of sage Atri and his disciple. I have embarked on a journey of enlightenment to learn from the wonders of *Nature*. My father has ordered me to go into the wide world and seek knowledge from *Nature*. I am in search of such knowledge. I thought of studying the *Panchabhootas* first and as a result, just completed my study of the earth and thereupon learned plenty of valuable lessons."

"That was quite nice of you to learn about the *Panchabhootas*. I am **Vayu** (Air), *God of the Winds*. I will tell you all about myself if you care to listen", said the stranger.

"Pray tell me your attributes", said Datta, humbly bowing before him with folded hands. True to his nature, the *God of the Winds* was moving around the place not remaining stationary in a single place. He was swirling all around the place. True to his name. he was as fickle as the wind.

* * *

"I am the God of the Winds. I change my form frequently according to the need. At times I am gentle and soothing; at other times, Nature may not be able to face my fury when I change into a gale. I have no particular form. I am present everywhere. Do you know that I am present inside you as your Internal Air or **Prana*** and externally in the outside world as the atmospheric air that blows all around you."

"Please tell me all about the Prana and what you do to help man", requested Datta.

"I am present in all living beings as the **Pancha Prana** (five vital life forces). They are respectively the **Prana, Apana, Vyana, Udana** and **Samana**. These are the five life forces or the Vital Airs in each living being. I will explain them in detail."

"The **Prana Vayu** is the life force, the air that moves into the body through the nostrils and reaches the lungs. It is also the force that helps intake of food (swallowing). When man learns to balance the Pranas, that is, balance the air coming in and going out through the nostrils, he learns to calm his mind and control his emotions. This you should learn from me. When we say Prana Vayu, we mean the air that enters the chest when we inhale."

"**Apana Vayu** is the air that pushes out the excretions from the body through the excretory and reproductive organs. It also controls the process of elimination through the pores in the body. When man controls the Apana Vayu, his digestive system is balanced. So is his reproductive system."

"**Vyana Vayu** is that which spreads from the heart and lungs to all parts of the body, thus circulating the life force throughout the body for the proper functioning of all the body systems and organs. It spreads the nutrients throughout the body."

"**Udana Vayu** is the air that we exhale. It moves upward from the lungs and helps speech and also helps the proper functioning of the brain and memory."

"**Samana Vayu** is present spiraling around the navel and helps in the churning and digestion of food. It can be balanced by proper eating habits."

"In short, Prana brings the fuel into the body, Samana converts this into energy, Vyana distributes this energy to the different systems of the body and Apana helps in eliminating the waste products of this metabolic process. Udana helps to manage the energy thus created by supplying it to the brain and other vital areas."

"I provide the air for the Pancha Pranas in the body of all living beings. For this I require very little energy from food. Hence the wise men understand that they have to consume only very little food barely necessary to keep the five Pranas working in a balanced manner. The wise man learns to control his Pranas by regular practice of Pranayama* which properly balances the Prana. Any excesses in food unbalances the Pranas and upsets the Pranic balance of the body. A balanced Prana in the body contributes to the healthy body of all living beings. Hence understand that the consumption of food should be only to keep one's Prana functioning and any excesses will be detrimental to the body. As the vital force or Prana, I keep the body and soul together. When at the end of life, the soul leaves the body, I no longer enter the body to perform my duty. That is when people say that the person's Prana has left the body forever."

"I am unseen but felt to the sense of touch. You can feel my presence even though you cannot see me. I am always free and move wherever and whenever I want. I am not bound by anyone or anything. Likewise, wisemen and saints understand that they should be free in this world and not bound to any place or person. The Universal Consciousness or the Brahman* is similarly Unseen and All-Pervasive like the Air and has to be **realized** and not **seen**."

"There are many things that man should learn from me. I help the other elements and all living beings through my external form. I help the trees and plants on earth by wafting the pollen from their flowers helping them to develop their fruits and seeds for perpetuating themselves in this world. I am the vital force in all animals, birds and even the minutest of living forms."

"I blow away any malodourous scent in the atmosphere and spread the sweet fragrance of flowers and plants throughout the atmosphere giving a pleasing sensation to all the life on earth. I waft away the smoke created by fire and help to soothe the bodies of all living beings scorched by the sun's rays. I provide the medium in the sky for the birds to fly about. For, without my support the birds will not find support in the sky. The clouds find space in the sky, but it is I who carry them across the seas and the continents to bring rain equally to all living beings in the world. And I never stake my claim to doing it or expect a reward for my actions."

"Know that in spite of all this, I never attach myself permanently to any of these – whether it be the sweet fragrances, the malodors, or the birds and insects that flit about in the sky. I am never **attached** to any of them. I only establish a temporary relationship with them and let go without any permanent bondage. A wise man also is like me. He learns to have relationships with people and material objects in life, but none of these are be permanent. He does not fall prey to attachment in life and learns to remain detached from material pleasures and bondage."

"I constantly keep moving all around. Seldom can you find me stationary. Continuous movement is my characteristic. The human mind is also like me. Very fickle and flitting from one thought to another. The wise man learns to control the mind to avoid it drifting into various thoughts and wandering all around like me. Hence, the wise should learn to control the mind and not allow it to wander like the wind."

* * *

Datta bowed before the *God of the Winds* again and thanked him for the enlightening words of wisdom. "I am now convinced that I have learned a lot from you today and how a wise man should live in this world detached from the material world. I shall practice this in my life in my aspiration to attain the state of an *Avadhoota*."

Detachment was an important lesson learnt from the Air. Saints should be **Free** and **Unbound** like the Air and **Never Permanently Attached**. They should be able to **move about freely** in the world like the ubiquitous Air. The **Brahman** is like **Prana**, present in all living beings, *unseen* but *felt*. These were the lessons that Datta learned from the Air.

Datta realized that he must have dozed off leaning against the tree. As it was growing dark, he decided to retire for the night and not to proceed further. He found a clean spot under a spreading *Neem** tree and settled down. A small rivulet gurgled beside the tree. He quenched his thirst and ate a couple of fruits that he had carried with him. Taking out his palm leaf scripts he began recording his exploits regarding the guidance he had received from Vayu, the God of the Winds.

Datta's observations - Summary

AIR

Amidst every life form, Prana weaves its spell,
Invisible, but its presence we can surely tell.
Unbound, unrestrained, Air roams the earth,
Aiding fruits, seeds, and trees with its gentle mirth.

Wind whispers through the trees, a pollinator's grace,
Spreading fragrance and cleansing in every place.
It lifts birds on its back, guiding them high,
And carries rain clouds through the boundless sky.

Ever transient, Air teaches the wise,
Letting go of attachments, learning to rise.
Like the mind, it flits with a fleeting art,
To master one's thoughts, a crucial part.

So, embrace the wisdom from *Nature's* cue,
Control the mind, and let the soul renew.
In every breath, the secrets lie,
To find serenity, let the winds be your guide.

SKY

As he sat, relaxing and munching on the luscious fruit, he observed the sky. The **Sky** or **Space** was the third of the *Panchabhootas*. The blue sky festooned with white fluffy clouds provided a canopy above. As he gazed at the sky, he wondered what the sky would tell him. Birds returning to their nests flew about in the sky screeching and hooting. As he watched, the sun descended in the horizon and the whole sky was painted with a magnificent orange hue as if it were on fire, taking his breath away. There seemed to be a play of colours in the horizon as the sky seemed to chase the setting sun into the depths of the ocean that stood far away. He could hear the birds chirping and cawing as they settled on the branches of the trees to retire for the night. Far away he could hear the whistling of a broad winged hawk that was flying high in the sky. The squawking of ravens could be heard nearby as they alighted on the branches of the tree under which Datta was resting.

Soon the sounds of the birds quietened down as the sky became dark as night set in. The silvery moon rose in the night sky and Datta noticed a few bright stars open their twinkling eyes to welcome the night. Having eaten the fruit and drunk the water from his water pot, Datta decided to settle for the night with his bundle of clothes doubling up as his pillow. Soon the whole world around him fell silent as he was swept into the arms of undisturbed slumber.

A whispering sound woke him up from his slumber. Looking around he found no one. The dark emptiness surrounded him. He could hear a distinct voice from the darkness, but he could see no one. Someone was calling his name, "Datta, Datta," the voice called out, but Datta could see no one.

"Who is it? Who are you? Show yourself," Datta challenged, "Are you hiding behind the trees? Come out, I cannot see you."

A deep baritone male voice said, "I am the **Akash** (Sky), the *God of the Skies*. You cannot see me as my main attribute is *'emptiness'*. I am all around you. I am **Space**."

Datta looked all around him but saw no one. "I cannot see you", he repeated.

"No, you cannot see me as I am invisible. I am the **Sky** or **Space**. I am the space that holds everything in the Universe. I have been ordained to help you understand me, know more about me and my endowments."

"Pray tell me about yourself and what I can learn from you," said Datta bowing his head to the unknown entity that was speaking to him.

* * *

"I am the all-pervading Sky or Space. I am inside and outside of everything in the Universe. I am inside all the living beings and surround all the objects in the universe. Everything in the Universe rests in me and I am part of everything. I support everything in my emptiness – the sun, the moon, the stars, the planets and all the living and non-living things therein. I am unconfined and without boundaries. You cannot see my beginning or my end. I am Infinity like Time."

"I do not have a form or odor. I am beyond recognition by the ordinary senses of living beings. I cannot be touched, tasted, smelt, heard, or seen as I am empty. You can see me as the sky with a blue color when I reflect the color of the ocean, when dark clouds gather in the space that I provide, I appear dark and during the twilight, I light up with various colours. But know that I have no color by myself. Thus, I clothe myself in different hues, but in the true sense, I have no color of my own. Lighting, thunder, and storms develop in my space, but I am free of their effects as they are temporary and soon pass."

"I provide the platform for the birds in the sky and the tiny insects like butterflies, bees, moths, and all air borne creatures space to carry out their activities and enjoy their frolicking. Occasionally, sandstorms and dust laden winds mar my vision, but they too are ephemeral and do not affect my basic nature."

"Know me, for nothing can exist without me for I provide the space for everything. Just as the fish cannot exist without water, nothing in the universe can exist without me. But at the same time, I never get attached to any of them, nor does anything leave an impression on me permanently. I provide support and accommodate the beautiful rainbows which the rain clouds bring in their wake. But they too are transient and leave no lasting impression on me."

"Understand that I am like the immutable Brahman, the Absolute Supreme Consciousness that governs every activity in the universe and provides sustenance for everything. Wise men understand that the Brahman is Omnipresent – both inside and outside, like me. They recognize the all-pervasiveness of the Brahman by looking at my nature and attributes. The Brahman is present in every life form in the universe both inside as the **Soul** or **Jeevatma** and outside as the omnipresent consciousness. Just as the Brahman which resides inside every living being as the **Atman**, I am also present inside and outside every living creature on earth. The wise sages realize this truth and understand the nature of the Brahman through my example."

"Know the greatness of the Brahman from me. Just as I have no attachment or relationship with the clouds that float in me or the stars and heavenly bodies that are accommodated by me, the Brahman also, even though it is present in all living beings as its Atman, has no attachment or relationship to the body."

"When a pot made of clay exists as a whole, I am present inside the pot and assume the shape and size of the pot. But when the pot of clay breaks, I merge with the space outside, with the vastness of the sky and am no longer confined. Similarly, understand that the Brahman also which is present in the body as the Atman merges with the Universal soul when the body disintegrates (dies). Brahman is all-pervading and at the same time confined in individual bodies as the Jeevatma. Thus, realize that the Absolute Consciousness is also like the unboundedness of the sky and space. Brahman also is not attached to anything even though everything rests within the Brahman. Thus, realize that the Supreme Personality is One and the only entity, and all the Jeevatmas are only reflections of the that entity."

"The wise sage learns this from the Sky and Space and realizes the greatness and the universality of the Brahman. This is the lesson that you must learn from me. Just as I do not mingle with all that I support, the self-realized sage also does not attach his mind to the emotions and Dvandvas*. The wise and the saintly do not attach themselves to any of the worldly objects that surround them and remain aloof from them as I do. They take a leaf out of my character and learn to accept joy and sorrow, pain and pleasure, praise, and censure all with the same equanimity like me. Even though I support the sun, the sun's heat does not affect me, even though I am heavily laden with clouds, the rain does not drench me, even though the storms and thunder occur in me, they do not affect me. So also, the wise men learn to be detached from the material pleasures and pains of this mundane life without being affected by them."

"This is the lesson that the wise learn from me."

* * *

Datta awoke the next day to the sweet chirping of sparrows on the branch of the tree that he slept under. He welcomed the sweet aroma of the flowers in the bushes around the clearing where he lay. A couple of squirrels were scurrying along looking for nuts or other edible fruits. Datta saw a tree laden with ripe bananas not far away from where he stood. He decided to collect his quota of food from there.

The whole episode of the previous night flashed before him like a dream. He was not sure whether it was a dream or his imagination. He decided to record his observations and inferences before embarking on his journey for the day.

Datta realized that the **Sky was All pervasive like the Brahman**, present inside and outside all beings. It supported everything being **Unattached** or **Unbound** by them. Sandstorms and squalls, lighting and thunder all occurred in the Sky. But left **No Impression** on the Sky. The wise too do not attach themselves to the transient emotions like **Love and Hate, Pain and Pleasure, Victory and Defeat** and consider them ephemeral and liable to pass.

<u>Datta's observations - Summary</u>

SKY (SPACE)

In boundless realms, the Sky holds all in grace,
With Sun, Moon Stars, adorning its embrace.
Yet ne'er confined, they dance in vast expanse,
Unshackled from its infinite advance.

Within, without, the Universe finds room,
Dark clouds and thunderstorms pain skies in gloom.
Rainbows arise, a sight both rare and true,
But sky, untouched, retains its azure hue.

Birds and butterflies, they freely roam,
Within its realm, they find their cherished home.
Supporting all, yet mingling not its essence,
Sky mirrors *Brahman's* boundless luminescence.

Learn from above, the wisdom it imparts,
Detachment from the world, the key to hearts.
Boundless, unbounded, it remains aloof,
Like Sky, find peace, and worldly woes stay aloof.

WATER

Datta observed that the summit of the mountain was not far away, and he would reach the summit in perhaps another hour. He gathered his belongings and using his *danda* as a support began climbing the last stretch of mountainous terrain that would lead him to the summit of the mountain.

Finally, he reached the crest of the mountain and looked around. It was flat like a tabletop and in one corner he found a clearing with a pool of fresh water. It was a mountain spring of crystal clear water which was gurgling up from the depths and flowing out into a small stream. The stream flowed down the side of the mountain. The surroundings were strewn with rocks and there were a few trees around the pool giving the whole area the appearance of a pleasant harborage where he could rest awhile. The sun was reaching overhead, and the heat was unbearable. Datta decided to rest and partake of his frugal lunch till the heat subsided before commencing his onward journey downhill. He sat on a patch of grass under the shade of a large tree and ate a couple of fruits and quenched his thirst from the waters of the wellspring. He wondered how the wellspring situated at this great height on the top of the mountain, not easily accessible to man or animals, could be of help to anyone. He decided to rest awhile and leaned against a boulder thinking of where his adventure would lead him next. He had learnt a lot from the Earth, Air, and the Sky. He stared at the pellucid water of the pool and thought that he should contemplate about the next *Panchabhoota* which was water. The cool breeze blowing from the west soothingly caressed his body.

A swishing sound made him turn towards the noise. A beautiful maiden stood there wearing flowing robes of white silk. Her garment was billowing and undulating around her buffeted by the breeze. The damsel had a tiara of shining diamonds atop her head and eardrops of shining pearls that glittered in the bright sun. A lingering smile quivered in her lips. She seemed to float about the place as she spoke in a sweet melodious voice.

"Datta, I know that you are in search of Self-realization and Truth in the world. I am **Ganga*** , the *Goddess of the Rivers*. **Water** is my essence. You know very well that Water forms the fourth of the *Panchabhootas* and is a very important ingredient for the sustenance of life."

Datta, stood up and with folded hands bowed before her. "My obeisance to you *Mother Ganga*. I am blessed by your presence. Yes, I am in search of the meaning of life and the lessons from *Nature*. I beseech you to enlighten me with your attributes. Pray tell me about your inherent nature."

* * *

"Listen, my dear Datta. I represent **Water** which is the fourth of the Panchabhootas and am pure and clean in my original state. My main Dharma is to **Purify** and **Clean**. Whomsoever I touch becomes clean and pure. In the process, I remove the contaminants from them. That is why I am revered by the saints as the remover of sins. I never discriminate between any of the living beings. I quench their thirst whoever they are. The animals, the birds, the plants, and trees all quench their thirst partaking of me. I am the essential element sustaining life and all life sprung from me at the beginning of creation. There cannot be life on this earth without me."

"Saints and wise men are like water. Whenever they come in contact with others, they purify their minds with their knowledge and advice. The Satsangs of saints chasten the mind of man like water removes the dirt from the body. Whomsoever a saint blesses, becomes pure. Saints remove the sins from individuals and show them the path to salvation. Saints and wise men, like water, do not discriminate among people. They treat everyone alike and help them irrespective of who they are. I serve all living beings in this world. Likewise, the saints serve all persons whether they are good or evil."

"By nature, I am **Transparent**. Know that the saints and the wise are also transparent in their behaviour and interactions with other humans. They never disguise their thoughts when interacting with other people. Purity of mind is a characteristic which they have imbibed from me. They never harbor any ill-will, negative feelings, or hatred in their mind against anyone. Even if a person harms or hurts them, the saint's behaviour towards them is kind and benevolent."

"I am sweet to taste when I am not contaminated by any external substances. Similarly, the saint attracts everyone with his sweet speech and behaviour. A saint's speech is like the vibrations that I create when I am in a cataract, the sea, or the brook. When faced with injustice, the wise man does not hesitate to rise to the occasion by speaking up against it like the roar of a cataract. When speaking with Saatwic persons, he is gentle like the swishing of the waves in the ocean. When interacting with children, the wise man becomes a child laughing and playing with them like the gurgling brook. The vibrations that he creates are always pleasing to the senses of whoever confronts him."

"I never expect anything back from nature or from any living being or man when I serve them. Unfortunately, man is not as thankful to me. He pollutes my waters with whatever he sees as waste. He never considers my pure nature. My ponds, wells and rivers are polluted beyond comprehension by the destructive activities of man. He never endeavors to help me maintain my purity and cleanliness. Man does not help me maintain the ecological balance in Nature. He even throws corpses into my waterbodies and violates me. But in spite of all this, I continue to serve man to the best of my ability as my Dharma always is to **Purify** and **Clean**."

"The saints recognize this great virtue of mine and take special care to revere me and avoid desecrating my purity. A wise man learns from me this nature of selfless service without expecting anything in return. I serve all irrespective of their caste, creed, race, or origin. When I plunge from the heaven as rains, I do not discriminate between individuals or regions. My rain drenches the deserts, the mountains, the plains, the forests, and the oceans alike. The wise man also does not discriminate people whatever be their position in life."

"The wise man recognizes the nature of the Supreme Consciousness or the Brahman knowing well that we are all part of the Brahman even though we are individual Jeevatmas. The rivers, the brooks, the streams, and the cataracts that carry water ultimately end up in the great ocean and once I reach the ocean, I lose my identity to merge with the one large ocean. The wise men realize this from me and know that the individual souls of humans too have to ultimately merge with the Brahman when they attain Moksha (salvation)."

"When the sun shines on my waterbodies, I rise up high into the heavens. I linger there for some time like the souls of living beings that rise up to occupy the astral worlds temporarily till they reincarnate back on earth. I take the form of clouds and travel across the skies with the help of the wind and reincarnate in another region or country as rain. Understand that I too follow the birth-death cycle and reincarnate as rain to help the living beings on earth. The sages and the wise men understand this aspect of Samsara (birth-death cycle) and strive towards salvation at the end of their lives."

"I bear the singular nature of assuming the form of the vessel or receptacle where I am held. When in a tiny Kamandalu, I assume its shape. When in a large pond, I assume a larger shape. In a river or ocean, I am larger. Thus, I am both **Flexible** and **Adaptable**. A saint, like me, learns to adapt to any circumstance in life. He is comfortable in the luxury of the palace of a king or the hut of a potter. He is never carried away by the luxury of the palace or worried by the inadequacies of the hut. He maintains the sang froid in whichever situation he finds himself. He maintains a balanced mind wherever he is. He takes after me in that."

"I always strive to move forward. Look at the rivers, they constantly move forward, whatever be the circumstances. A river cannot flow back. Every moment it keeps moving forward. The wise man is like this. He moves forward, always living in the present. He does not waste his time brooding on the past or on his sorrows and ruminating on them. He learns to forget and forgive the past hurts and insults and moves forward constantly like the river."

"I am always **Humble** seeking to flow to lower levels and never proud or arrogant. The greater I become like the wide river or the mighty ocean, the lower I am compared to the other water bodies. The enlightened saint is also like me. The greater his knowledge and wisdom, the humbler and more unpretentious he is. . He never becomes arrogant or proud and is content to keep a low profile like the ocean."

"Some of my water bodies like a pond or a pool in the confines of the compound of a person may be of use only to one person or a few people. But when I flow as a river, I bring solace and succour to a large number of people in the form of drinking water, irrigation, and comfort. Saints are also like rivers. They are not like ponds which serve a limited number of people but are like the river useful and beneficial to the whole society."

* * *

Datta awoke with a start. It appeared that he had been daydreaming. The hot sun above and the cool breeze blowing from the west had lulled him into a languor and may be he dreamt about the *Goddess Ganga*. But inspired by the occurrence, he began to record this in his palm leaf manuscript.

Purity and **Cleanliness** were the main attributes of Water. The **Transparent** nature of water was like the open mind of saints and the wise which did not hide their thoughts, or harbor ill will against anyone. Their words were **Sweet** like pure water, and they **Never Discriminate** like water. As all the flowing waters reach the vast ocean, all souls ultimately merge with the **Brahman** in Moksha. Just like water, the wise and the saintly are **Flexible** and **Adaptable** to any situation. **Humility** is their nature, like water.

Datta's observations   -   Summary

WATER

In the realm of Water's grace, we find,
A cleansing force both pure and kind.
Life's essence it sustains and cares,
Quenching thirst, each form it bears.

No bias shown to rich or poor,
It serves all souls, forever more.
As saints like Water, souls they mend,
With every meeting, hearts they tend.

Words of the wise, like waters sweet,
Revive the souls, they chance to meet.
From vapors high to rains below,
Desert and forest, life will grow.

In selflessness, like waters flow,
The saints, with love, their virtues show.
Just as all waters find the sea,
Souls merge with *Brahman*, pure and free.

Rivers flow forward, seeking low,
Present and humble, saints bestow.
Selflessly serving, with hearts so true,
Like water's course, they renew.

So, let us learn from Water's role,
To cleanse, sustain, and make us whole.
Embrace the *Dharma* of water's might,
And live like saints, with love and light.

FIRE

A pall of clouds had masked the sun, Datta decided to continue his journey before the sun set and reach a safe place for him to sojourn for the night. He set forth with his bundle and *danda* after collecting a few fruits and water from the wellspring.

He decided to follow the stream which flowed from the wellspring down the mountain. From atop the mountain, he saw a village far away. The stream meandered through the gorge on the side of the mountain and flowed down. Datta began walking beside the stream.

He descended the rather easy terrain and began moving towards the foot of the mountain. The valley was visible below. He decided to spend the night in the valley. He followed the gurgling stream which seemed to expand in size as it flowed downhill. As Datta neared the foot of the mountain, he saw the ruins of an old temple with a *mandapam* (porch ; vestibule) in front. He decided to rest there for the night. The stream had by now widened into a small river and flowed near the ruins of the temple. He could see the outskirts of the village far away.

Datta placed his bundle of belongings, *danda* and *Kamandalu* on the *mandapam* and went to the river to have a dip. He felt the soothing coolness of the river after having travelled in the scorching sun the whole day. The sun was approaching the horizon and the heat had subsided. Having bathed, Datta completed his *Sandyavandanam* (evening prayers) and returned to the *mandapam*. The sun had not set yet. As he was preparing to settle down and eat the fruits that he had collected from the mountain, he heard the voice of a group of people approaching singing hymns of Sri Rama. Soon they rounded the corner in a narrow path that seemed to come from the village. Four villagers wearing turbans were carrying a bier with a corpse shrouded from head to foot in a red cloth. Datta recognized that this was the body of a woman whose husband was still alive. Only a *Sumangali's* (woman with husband alive) corpse is shrouded in red cloth. Men's and widow's corpses are shrouded in a white cloth. In front of the bier, walked a man with tonsured head carrying an earthen pot from which smoke was billowing out. Obviously, it was the **Agni** (Fire) for lighting the pyre. The *Agni* would have been taken from a *homam* (fire ritual) conducted at the home of the deceased and the man carrying it would obviously be the husband of the woman who had died. He wore a single loin cloth dripping with water, having bathed in the river before coming the ghat to cremate his deceased wife. Behind the bier were many men who had accompanied the body to partake in the cremation rituals.

In a distance, by the banks of the river, Datta saw four men setting up the pyre with a pile of firewood and dried cow dung cakes. Datta decided to watch the rituals and moved closer to where the pyre was being set up. The men carrying the body on a bier made of bamboo poles tied together in the form of a ladder, placed the bier along with the body on top of the pyre. The priest who was with the husband intoned the chant for performing the funeral rites in a singsong tone and this was repeated by the husband. Then he went around the pyre thrice with a pot of water on his right shoulder from which water poured out through a hole in a thin stream around the pyre.

Mandapam

After three such circumambulations, he dropped the pot behind him, which stuck a rock and broke into pieces. Next, the husband emptied the pot with the Agni on the chest of the body of the deceased. Those who accompanied him fanned the flames which soon picked up into a roaring conflagration assisted by adding a vessel of ghee to the pyre. The people who accompanied the funeral procession helped to stoke the fire and soon the pyre was a raging inferno.

All the people who had partaken in the funeral returned along with the husband without once looking back, as is the custom in many Hindu communities. Datta stood a little away from the funeral pyre mumbling the *Maha Mrithyunjaya mantra** for the emancipation of the soul of the deceased. He stood there looking at the raging fire for some time and then moved towards the river to take a dip. As he had partaken in the cremation ritual, though from a distance, he had to take a bath, as is the custom, to cleanse himself before the evening meal.

Datta settled down on the wide parapet that ran all around the large *mandapam* which was supported by granite pillars with exquisite sculptures of various gods, animals, and birds. He admired the architecture of the *mandapam* as he ate his supply of fruit and drank water from his *Kamandalu*. Using the bundle of clothes as his pillow, he decided to rest for the night.

There was a gentle breeze blowing from across the river which stoked the pyre into a great blaze which lit up the whole area. The wood burned with a crackling sound as the twigs broke apart in the heat and the flames and sparks leapt up as if to reach for the sky. The orange tongues of flames reminded him of the thousand headed snake *Ananthan* on which *Bhagavan Vishnu* lay in the milky ocean.

A soft sound woke him up from his reverie. Before him stood a tall elderly man in flaming orange colored robe which flapped around the in the cool breeze of the night. His eyes were red, and his ruddy complexion enhanced his sharp features. A crown of red rubies adorned his head, and he held a helical staff in his hand. His majestic figure was one which inspired awe and respect at the same time.

Datta stood up in reverence and bowed before the figure recognizing him to be a divine being, but not knowing who he was.

"I am **Agni**, *The God of Fire,* said the apparition. I am the fifth element of the *Panchabhootas*. I reckon you have met with the other four already. Word is about that you are in search of knowledge from *Nature* which will lead you to self-realization to become an *Avadhoota* and I am here to help you understand my nature – the nature of **Agni** or **Fire**.

* * *

Agni continued, *"Unlike the other elements of the Panchabhootas, I have two special characteristics. I provide both* **Light** *and* **Heat**. *Occasionally, I am seen as a blazing fire visible to everyone. At times I hide myself as smoldering embers and conceal myself beneath a blanket of ashes. The wise and saintly men also are like me. They conceal their true knowledge and saintly features at times hide their power and potential brilliance beneath a blanket of humility and appear as simpletons or may even appear crazy. Only when required does their true didactic knowledge get revealed. Have you not heard the story of Jadabharatha who was going about the world as a dunce and was considered a lunatic by society, till one day the king happened to cross his path and Jadabharatha revealed himself to the king as an all-knowing sage?"*

"At other times, I blaze forth with my thousand tongues of flame like the veritable saints who bless the world with their knowledge and prowess. I consume everything that is given to me with the same impartiality and convert them ultimately into ashes. The end product is always ash. Just as the whole universe ultimately is one Supreme Consciousness – the **Brahman**.*"*

"I have no **Form** *or* **Shape** *of my own and so, rightly assume the form of whichever substance or material that I combust. I can burn as a large conflagration when I consume a whole forest and incinerate large stretches of grassland. But I can also burn as a simple light-giving flame in an oil lamp with a tiny wick. Saints are also like me. They can be profound like me or be subdued like the tiny flame in a lamp. Understand that the Jeevatma also has no form of its own. It assumes the physical form into which it has*

entered be it a bird, an animal, a tree, or a human being. Even though I consume anything and everything that I come into contact with, I remain ever **Pure** without being contaminated. Be it a corpse or a log of sandalwood, everything is the same for me like the saint who would not discriminate between the different material objects in the universe."

I digest everything put into me. All the offerings given unto me are consumed and equally digested by me without any discrimination. I accept pure and impure substances into me and digest them without getting contaminated myself. So are saintly individuals. They partake of any food given to them without any preferences or choice. To them all are the same. I am the **Jatharagni*** within all living beings. The Jatharagni in saints is so powerful that they can digest anything given to them. Even contaminated food or poison is digested by the sage without ill effects. This metaphorically means that the sages and wise men are immune to any adverse comments, insults, indignity or blasphemy and accept the good and bad with equanimity. To them, anything is welcome, they accept and assimilate it. All the inauspicious and negative tendencies get torched by the saint's austerity and does not affect him at all. Know this from the story of sage Agasthya and the Rakshasa brothers Vathapi and Ilvala*."

"I give warmth to all alike when it is cold. I never discriminate between the rich and the poor, the prince, and the pauper or the Brahmana* and the Sudra* when it comes to providing light and heat. I treat all God's creations equally. The truly enlightened sage also does not distinguish between individuals based on which Varna* he belongs to. The Avadhoot who sees the Brahman in everything in the universe does not distinguish between the God's creations on

69

earth. To him, the Jeevatma in the elephant is the same as the one in the ant."

"Often, I am latent in substances like wood or rock and my presence is known only when subject to agitation as when two pieces of rock or metal strike each other or when the woods in the forest rub against each other to spark a conflagration. Till then I remain dormant and latent, invisible to anyone. Many saints are also like me that they do not go around exposing their knowledge and prowess, but when the circumstances demand, they come out with their knowledge and wisdom to help mankind overcome their Karmas and attain Moksha."

"I am always **Pure** and **Purify** things which associate with me. Gold gets purified when it comes into contact with me. The impurities get burned off and pure gold emerges. Saints are also pure like me. They are free of sins and any negative tendencies are destroyed in the fire of their austere nature. Also, when people come into contact with saints and wise men, their negative proclivities and evil propensities get destroyed and they become Sattvic and absolved of their sins."

* * *

Datta suddenly woke up to find that it had grown very dark. The moon was well above the horizon and shining brightly as a lunar crescent. What had happened seemed to be a dream, but he decided to make a detailed transcript of the observations the next day when he woke up. He reflected on the dream that he had about ***Agni***, the God of Fire and pondered over the conversation that he had. Recollecting the details, he fell asleep.

Datta realized that Agni gave **Light** and **Heat** to anyone without discrimination. Fire had no **Form** or **Shape** and assumed the shape of whatever it burns like the **Jeevatma** assumes the form of whichever living form it enters into. Agni is **Latent** in wood and stone like the knowledge inherent in the wise and the saintly. In all living beings it is present as the **Jatharagni** which metabolizes food to provide nourishment to the body. Agni **Purifies** substances like gold and brings out their pure and lustrous nature. Likewise, saints tend to destroy the negative and evil tendencies in people whom they come into contact with.

Datta's observations - Summary

FIRE

In brilliant blaze, both heat and light,
Fire dances, flames a glorious sight.
Overt, blazing, or embers low,
Concealing its power, till it must show.

Unbiased it consumes all's fair,
Reducing all to ashes bare.
Assuming forms of what it burns,
Like souls that wander, fate's concerns.

Unblemished, saints, like Fire, stand tall,
Untouched by insults, bitter thrall.
No discrimination in its pyre,
Between the wicked and the saintly sire.

Present in all, life's sacred art,
Jatharagni, the Fire in every heart.
Purifying gold with righteous glee,
Saints purify souls, setting them free.

MOON

The cool night breeze was soothing. It carried the fragrance of the *Champaka* (magnolia) flowers from the tree that stood nearby. This gave Datta a feeling of peace and joy. What a beauty nature was! *Nature's* bounty assailed one's senses and gave pleasure and tranquility to the ruffled mind. He realized how the lingering redolence of the flowers hypnotized his intellect into creativity. He stared at the **Moon** which shone high above the clouds. It seemed to play hide and seek behind the clouds and occasionally smiling brightly at him. It looked as if the moon was beaming at his discomfiture.

Someone was calling his name softly, "Datta, Datta...."

He looked around but saw no one. His name was called again, and he turned to see behind him a tall handsome youth with an alabaster complexion smiling at him. His silvery robes added charm to his beauty. He wore a crown on his forehead studded with precious moonstones and a long string of pearls hung from his neck. His lips were red, and his dark eyes appeared to be lined with kohl. His body was visible only up to his waist and the lower part of the body appeared to be shadowed.

Datta recognized him as a divine being, probably, a demi god and quickly stood up and bowed before him. "Pray tell me who you are", he said with folded hands, "I do not recognize your divine self."

"I am **Chandra**, the *God of the Moon*. I have been directed by *Indra*, the God of the Heavens to come and speak to you and enlighten you on my role and give you advice regarding what lessons I can impart you."

* * *

"I wax and wane during the month and you can see my brightness in the sky diminishing and expanding every fortnight. But really, I am whole and maintain my lunar globe under all circumstances. Saints learn this from me. The body undergoes metamorphosis during life from childhood, through adolescence and adulthood to senescence. This is influenced by Time which controls everything in the universe. But the soul within the body – be it human or any other living being- does not undergo any change at all."

"Similarly, in a person's life, there are pain and pleasure, there are periods of depression and periods of happiness. Nothing is permanent. There are ebbs and flows in life and man should learn to accept both with equanimity. The saints have learnt this from me, and they face the

vicissitudes of life and the good and bad times in life with equal tranquility. The wise never get disturbed by the pin pricks in life and do not get overly elated by the joyous achievements. The saints know how to remain balanced in all situations without losing their composure. This is the secret of life that the saints and the wise learn from me. Such a person is called a **Sthithaprajna***. So, am I. My brightness waxes and wanes, but I remain calm, collected, and whole always."

"At times, the clouds mar my countenance, but I am not bothered by them. The wise men also are thus not bothered by any heresies or praise heaped on them, as they know that like the waxing and waning of the moon, this too shall pass. They very well know that bad times roll in and roll out, but the saint never loses his level headedness under any circumstance. Know this from me. In your life you may have situations where you face praise and insult. When you are praised you feel happy, and your mind becomes enthusiastic, and you feel like working harder towards success. This even makes you yearn for praise. Isn't it so? Because praise is an aphrodisiac that makes you work harder and achieve more in life."

"But how do you face insults and criticism? When you face criticism, you should become more cautious. You should become additionally aware of your mistakes and shortcomings. You should take care to avoid mistakes from your side. So, whereas praise acts as an incentive and a catalyst, criticism and insults should act as means to make you more aware of your mistakes and shortcomings. They should act as learning experiences. So, when praise and insults assail you in life, understand that these are catalysts to your progress in one way or the other. If so, you will neither become devastated when you face criticism nor euphoric when you are applauded. Understand that <u>this phase also will eventually come to an end</u>."

If a person is always praised, he may not recognize any mistakes that he may commit. But if a person continually faces criticism, he may lose the will to work further due to lack of self-confidence. Thus, learn to convert your praise into encouragement for your success and convert the censures into positive didactic knowledge to correct yourself. If so, you will be able to go forward in life accepting both praise and censure dispassionately."

"Good and evil are the two facets of life. Both are important. Whereas goodness has to be practiced diligently and developed, evil grows of its own accord. Going up in life needs effort and will. But to fall in life, is easy. It is like rolling a stone uphill which is an arduous task, but the stone rolls downhill without any effort. One can easily fall into evil ways. It is like the weeds and garden plants. The gardener takes pains to sow the seeds of flowering and fruit bearing plants, prepare the soil, manure it water it and protect the plant against marauders to see it grow and bloom. But the weeds grow in the garden of their own accord without the need for any care, manuring or watering. So are weeds of evil tendencies in and individual."

"The universe is not bothered whether you are good or evil. The universe has no partiality towards good or evil. Just as it accepts night and day, it accepts evil and good. But being good is your need, not that of the universe. Because goodness is needed for your happiness and peace. Hence keep on trying to be good always. If you are lazy, evil grows in you by itself like weeds in the garden. Hence do not *be lazy in cultivating the goodness in you. It takes pains to be good. There is no use blaming evil or God in this matter. Because the need is yours. Hence understand that in this universe, both good and evil are like the two sides of a coin. A coin must have two sides. But both coexist. The Supreme Consciousness, however, is impartial and only a passive observer. The Universal Soul has no role in the good and evil nature of man. This is like the waxing and waning of the moon which you see every month in my appearance."*

"This life is a mixture of joys and sorrows. Life is to enjoy. Have you ever thought about this? Most people complain that they are not able to enjoy life and be happy. But think, if you are always happy, then a time will come when you will not recognize what happiness is. To know happiness, you must experience sorrow also from time to time. It is only when you are sad that you understand the true value of being happy. If you give food to someone who is suffering from hunger, his happiness will be boundless. But if you give food to someone who is fully satiated, he will not be happy with it. You gave the same food to both. But their responses will be different. The rich may not be happy with this, but the poor feel elated with the food that you give. Similarly, if you are full of happiness, you will not recognize its true value.

That is why it is said that both sorrows and happiness should be part of life like the sweet and the sour tastes in food. <u>It is the sorrow that heightens the value of happiness</u>. So, do not ignore sorrows from your life. Understand that sorrows are also part of your life. Know that sorrows are to make you aware of the intensity of happiness. <u>Realize that sorrows are the shadows of happiness</u>. If you are always sad, you will not understand the true value of happiness. Similarly, if you are always happy you will not understand what sorrow is. So, learn to accept both sorrow and happiness with equanimity. This state is called the state of **Sthithaprajna***."

"Thus, learn from me to face the Dvandvas* (opposites) in life. Whatever be the changes or reversals that you face in life, understand that this phase is only transient. All the rest are only phases of life that come and go."

* * *

The chirping of sparrows awoke Datta from his sleep. He realized that all that he saw was but a dream. But the profundity of the philosophical truths communicated to him by **Chandra**, *the God of the Moon* were deeply ingrained in his mind. He had to record them in his palm leaf manuscript. He took out his palm leaf manuscript from his bundle and began writing.

Datta realized that the **Body Changes** from childhood through youth to old age, like the waxing and waning phases of the Moon's brightness but the **Soul** within remains unchanged. The wise, the *Sthithaprajna* treat opposites like pain and pleasure alike. Joy and sorrow are part of life and both are needed for a balance in life. The wise learn to convert **Praise** into incentives and **Criticism** into guides for correcting themselves. **Happiness** cannot be relished if **Sorrow** is not experienced occasionally.

Datta's observations - Summary

MOON

In life's dance, the Moon, she seems to sway,
Through wax and wane, her form may change.
Yet whole, steadfast, she reigns by night and day,
A mirror to the soul, untouched, not estranged.

Saints serene, amidst life's joys and sorrows,
Embrace the lunar tides of fate's design.
With wisdom's grace, they face each morrow,
Knowing all shall pass, shifting sands benign.

Criticism's voice, a guide for the wise,
To better selves, they humbly tend.
Neither drunk on praise, nor downcast with lies,
In balanced hearts, humility ascends.

As good and evil entwine life's thread,
Two faces on a coin they appear.
One, a tender shoot, by nurture fed,
The other a weed, that spreads without fear.

To God all souls are equal, fair,
Whether steeped in virtue or vice's trance.
Through sorrows, joy gains meaning rare,
Two facets of life's fleeting dance.

Amidst these changes, the constant shore,
The Supreme Brahman, eternal and vast,
Beyond the ebb and flow, forevermore,
A beacon of truth, steadfast to the last.

SUN

The sun had not yet risen, and the day was just breaking. A streak of light in the horizon heralded the sunrise. Datta got up and went to the river to complete his ablutions and have his morning bath and his morning *Japa** and meditation. He needed an early start today and hoped to reach the village which he could see at a distance. He decided to spend the night at the village. Having partaken of a few sweet edible berries which he found in a bush nearby, Datta proceeded on his journey.

The sun had just cleared the horizon when Datta commenced his onward journey. With his bundle of belongings, he began the trek towards the remote village. He saw the early morning sun break through a pageant of grey clouds which were lazily floating by as if they had nothing else to do other than glide about. The rising sun shone against the blushing sky as an orange orb looking exquisitely beautiful.

Looking at the early morning sun, Datta was fascinated by the sun's effulgence. 'What a beautiful piece of creation, the **Sun** is', he thought. He could not but admire the magnificent sight of the sun rising beyond the mountain flooding the valley with its bounteous rays and bringing life to the region. He was sure that if he contemplated on the sun, he would learn more from the **Sun** and its distinct function in the tapestry of the universe.

He quickened his pace and continued to walk forward aiming to reach the village before sundown so that he could rest there for the night. It was noon and the sun was directly overhead. As Datta felt tired and hungry due to the scorching heat of the sun, he decided to rest under the sprawling banyan tree that invitingly stood at the outskirts of the village. The villagers had constructed a large parapet all around the base of the tree for itinerant travelers and workers to rest. That was also the place where the village council under the aegis of the village headman met once a month to discuss problems related to the village and administer justice whenever required. The village was the basic unit of society just like the family. Villages in ancient India were the pillars of society which decided on the day to day administration of societal matters.

Datta unloaded his bundle on to the parapet and sat down to partake of his frugal meal of fruits and water. Feeling tired owing to the scorching sun overhead, he decided to take a breather before going further towards the village. He sat under the cool shade of the tree and leaned against the tree and closed his eyes out of weariness.

The sound of horses hooves woke him up. He found a warrior like figure wearing a shiny suit of golden armor with a matching golden helmet and a shining spear in his right hand riding a chariot approaching him. The chariot was drawn by seven horses. The warrior wore a flaming orange cape which undulated in the breeze as he rode rapidly towards Datta. The fine golden filigree in the cape billowed around him like the rays of the sun giving him an aura of divinity. When he reached where Datta sat, he alighted from the chariot and strode towards Datta. Seeing him Datta rose from the parapet where he sat and accosted him. "O! mighty warrior, who are you? You look like a noble warrior from the king's court."

Banyan Tree

"I am **Surya**, the *Sun-God* said the stranger. I have been sent by *Indra* the God of the Heavens to counsel you. I was charged with the task of enlightening you on my duties in the universe and how the saints and savants draw inspiration from me."

* * *

"Saints and wise men learn from my characteristics and attributes. I will tell you about them now. I am the sole **Energy Provider** *to the whole world. Without me there would be no life forms on earth. I energize and sustain the entire world – the fauna and flora of the earth. The seasons change in the world because of my influence. I provide sustenance to all the plants and trees on earth by means of my radiance. The plants and trees on the other hand nourish the animals and other small creatures with their fruits and leaves. These creatures are in turn eaten by the carnivorous animals, and this keeps the ecological cycle going on earth. Man derives his energy from all these. Thus, you see that I provide the energy and nourishment to every life form in the world."*

"I suck the water from the various water bodies on earth including the mighty ocean and carry them into the clouds. From there, with the help of the wind, I dissipate them to various places as rain. I do not differentiate between regions or countries when I provide the rain. I am impartial in this matter. I do not distinguish between the good and the wicked or the righteous and the villainous when I provide sunshine to them. But in spite of all this I am not arrogant or proud that I am doing this for their benefit. I never am proud or haughty over my ability to do this. Saints and wise men are like me. They learn to do good and serve society without expecting anything in return. They share their knowledge with the people around and spread the light of enlightenment without expecting any profits or benefits. They shower their blessings on all and sundry like the cool rains that I bring to all people alike. But they never take pride on this or feel pretentious about it. They live lives of unimpeachable rectitude and integrity."

"I am the only one who provides **Light** and **Heat** to the whole world. But my reflections are seen in myriads of substances on earth, on water bodies, metals, and any other reflecting surface. I am mirrored in the crystal clear water of the Ganga and also in the dirty water in the drains. But I am untouched by any of these reflections. So also, the **Soul** which is housed in the living, be it a human or an animal or a bird or a tree is untouched by the characteristics of the body which it occupies. The **Soul** is ever pure and pervasive and does not have the attributes of the body."

"I am the one and only sun. saints and the wise men understand that I am like the Brahman. The Brahman is but one but is reflected in many bodies and living beings as different souls. This great truth is realized by the scholars and saints who, hence, treat all living beings alike. They see the oneness of the Supreme Being in all living creatures and all human beings whichever Varna, race, or ethnicity they belong to. They embrace the whole humanity and living beings as part of that one great truth. The soul is one, only the body is different. Only the foolish and the dim-witted think that each person is different from the other."

Datta learnt the importance of **Selfless Service** *and the* **Omnipotence** *of the Brahman from the Sun. The Sun is* **One like the Brahman** *but is reflected in myriad substances. The Sun provides* **Energy** *to all life forms on earth. It provides sunshine uniformly* **Without Discrimination***. So do the* **Wise** *and the* **Saintly** *who provide* **Knowledge** *and* **Advice** *to all.*

<u>**Datta's observations - Summary**</u>

SUN

In the heavens above, Sun's bright rays,
Sustains all life with its warm embrace.
Through seasons' dance, it influence sways,
Provider of energy, the world's saving grace.

In clouds it gathers waters wide,
Showering rain on both friend and foe.
With humility, it casts its pride,
A lesson for us it seeks to sow.

Saints like the Sun, selflessly give,
Spreading knowledge and guiding art.
Blessings showered, all hearts they sieve,
With love and kindness, they impart.

As Sun's light reflects in every place,
On water's surface and metal's sheen,
So does Atman, a divine embrace,
In living beings, untainted and serene.

The Soul, a unity that transcends,
Though bodies differ, it remains the same.
Boundless love, where all life descends,
In this grand cosmic dance, we find out aim.

PIGEON

Datta came out of his reverie to see that the sun was already approaching the horizon. He decided to press on and reach the village before the sunset. He accelerated his pace. As he approached the village, he saw a few village folk recognize him from the previous day's encounter at the burial ground. They ran to inform the chieftain in the village and soon a band of villagers under the leadership of the chieftain came to receive him at the outskirts of the village.

On seeing his charismatic countenance, they paid obeisance to him and accosted him. "O ! great saint", the headman spoke bowing humbly before him, "We are honored by your presence here in this humble village of ours. We welcome your presence to give us advice on spirituality and share *Satsang* with us during your stay with us. Please bless us and stay with us for a few days and enlighten our folk with your kind words of wisdom."

Datta smiled at the headman. He was pleased with their guileless nature. "I am but a mendicant, a *Sannyasi* traveling from place to place in search of knowledge. I myself am in search of knowledge from *Nature* after my education at the *Ashram* of sage Atri. I am his disciple. I am glad to stay with you for a few days and share what little knowledge I possess."

Word had already spread around the village and the men, women and children were lined on both sides of the street to welcome the 'traveling saint' as he was soon called. In spite of the chieftain's invitation to stay at his house, Datta opted to stay in the village *Satram* (<u>choultry</u> ; <u>caravansary</u>) along with other travelers. The chieftain ordered his subordinates to make all arrangements for Datta's stay.

Datta settled himself in the *Satram* and began teaching the villagers elements of spirituality. He would often engage the children in conversation and tell them parables from the *Puranas* and the epics in Hindu mythology. The children of the village loved him for his insightful stories. He endeared himself to the villagers who often visited him to get his advice on various matters regarding their personal problems and Datta was able to help them in sorting out their problems. The chieftain met him daily and discussed the problems that the village faced. For his part, Datta gave him sensible advice as to how he could solve them. His knowledge was expanding and Datta continued to mature in his pursuit of spiritual knowledge and blossom into a full-fledged saint. His ultimate aim was however, to become an *Avadhoota*.

Near the *Satram* stood a large mango tree laden with fruits. Many birds and tiny rodents like squirrels had made it their home. On a branch of the tree a couple of pigeons had built their nest. The couple were always together and Datta could see that they were greatly attached to each other.

Often they would sit on the branch of the tree and preen each other's feathers, cooing and fondling each other. They would go in search of food together. They would go to the nearby farm and peck at loose grains that lay scattered during the husking of the grain. Occasionally they would go to the pond near the *Satram* and have a dip in the cool waters and shake themselves free. They would fly around the place each chasing the other in a playful mood. It was obvious that they were overly devoted to each other.

Soon they built a large nest, and the female pigeon laid a few eggs in the nest. As days went by the eggs hatched and the tiny hatchlings came out with their screeching voices. The two parent pigeons would go out into the village and come back with food for their hatchlings. The tiny birds soon grew larger and learned to fly. They would flutter around the tree or swoop down occasionally to pick grains or morsels of food that the travelers discarded when they rested in the shade of the tree. The two parent birds were immensely fond of their little ones and openly displayed their affection by pampering them with food.

One day, a fowler happened to pass by and noticed the birds' nest and the little ones in it. Deciding to capture them, he rigged up a net below the tree and hid himself behind the *Satram*. The little birds were attracted by the tasty morsels of food that the fowler had scattered under the net so that they were soon pecking at it voraciously. While pecking at the morsels of food, the little pigeons did not realize that their feet had become entangled in the net, and they were trapped.

Soon the mother pigeon came to the nest with a morsel of food in its beak to feed its little ones and noticed to her horror that all her little ones were entangled in the net below. She could do nothing to save them and began flying around making shrieking noises of distress, but it was of no avail. Finally, out of sheer desperation, she landed on the net trying to free her little ones and she too was trapped in the net. The father bird which returned with food for the family found that his family was trapped in the fowler's net. It was helpless and unable to free the birds and in desperation landed on the net with the intention of saving the family, but unfortunately, it too became entangled in the net. The fowler who was watching this from afar ran to the net and captured all birds and caged them.

Datta felt deeply distressed on seeing this. But being a sannyasi, he did not interfere in the fowler's actions. He fell into a deep thought regarding the distress of the birds.

* * *

***Attachment is the root cause of misery.** The birds were too attached to each other and that was the reason for their grief. The fowler took advantage of this. He knew that if he captured the little pigeons, the parent birds would also get trapped in his net out of love for their little ones. Datta realized from the episode of the birds that in this world one should not be unduly attached to one's kith and kin.*

Man's attachment to material possessions often leads to severe disappointment and misery in life. Bondage as a result of attachment to individuals and one's family also leads to anguish. This does not mean that the Grihastha* should not love his family and provide for them. He should be **concerned** about them but not exceedingly **attached** to them emotionally. It is man's attachment that leads him to anguish. Excess attachment to the members of one's family leads to disastrous consequences to some when the member leaves them or dies. **Concern is normal, bondage is not.** Evil folk learn to take advantage of a person's attachment to possessions and his family and use it to achieve their own malicious ends.

Excess attachment to his son Duryodhana was the cause of the king Dhritarashtra's suffering. He had to see the death of all his hundred sons. Excess attachment to his wife Kaikeyi was the reason why King Dasaratha had to part with his sons Rama and Lakshmana. History is rife with incidents where excessive visceral attachment to one's family or kith and kin led to agony and distress.

Excessive attachment to wealth caused the downfall and decadence of many men in history. Attachment to land has landed many kings in misery. Attachment to power and prestige is also the source of despair to many.

From this man should learn that his attachment should not be to the material possessions and worldly pleasure, but the to the greater truth, the Absolute Consciousness or Brahman. This will lead to eternal happiness, bliss, and salvation.

One should be concerned and absorbed in the affairs of one's family but that should not lead to a permanent bondage to the detriment of his spiritual life. In the attachment to the family, one should not forget to pursue the spiritual truth that the body is impermanent, and the Soul is permanent. The ultimate aim of human existence is attaining Moksha.

Like the parent pigeons, in certain situations in life, we may have to take strong decisions. This may occur during various stages of our life. And these decisions may strongly influence our future. The decisions we take thus may be the cause of our future joy or sorrow. It may affect not only us but also our family and relatives too. Some decisions that we make may affect our future generations also. Why do we have to take such decisions? When we face a situation where a decision is to be made, our mind often gets filled with anxiety or fear. There is a battle of wits taking place inside our mind. This may be the time when we make wrong decisions like the parent birds did and hence were ensnared in the fowler's net.

Those who make decisions do it in two ways. One set of people will take a decision to solve the problem that is in front of them. The others take a decision to overcome the anxiety in their minds. The first group takes an **Intelligent Decision** whereas the second group takes an **Emotional Decision**. We tend to forget an important fact that has to be considered when deciding on something. <u>A decision should not be taken to assuage the anxiety in our mind temporarily</u>. Even if a decision does not give us immediate solace and calm our anxiety, it should not, in future, cause us sorrows. The decisions that we take should cause happiness to us in future.

* * *

These were the thoughts that ran through Datta's mind when he thought of the plight of the family of pigeons. Often life teaches us **Positive** lessons and at times **Negative** lessons. *It is important to know what to do in a* *situation, but equally important, it is to know what not to do.* **Attachment** is often the root cause of **Misery**. **Concern** for one's family is normal, **Bondage** is not. Attachment to ephemeral pleasures and worldly possessions should give way to attachment to the **Supreme Consciousness** which is *Brahman*. One should learn to take **Intelligent Decisions** and not **Emotional Decisions** in life. Emotional decisions often lead one to disaster and sorrow, whereas intelligent decisions lead one towards success and contentment.

Datta's observations - Summary

PIGEON

Love binds, but beware of misery's grasp,
Too much to kin, despair might soon unmask.
Family care is crucial, but not as chains,
For bonds to tight, heartache and grief remains.

Evil ones exploit possessions we keep,
To achieve wicked aims, they slyly creep.
Dhritarashtra's love brought Kuru's sad end,
A lesson learnt, to attachment, we must mend.

Attach to the Divine, for *Moksha's* light,
Release anxiety, make choices bright.
Let wisdom guide, not emotions blind,
In intelligent decisions, peace we find.

Emotions sway, a seed of future dole,
Sorrow averted when intelligence takes part.
In twelve lines' span, these lessons now resound,
In stanzas four, their wisdom we unbound.

PYTHON

Datta could not stay for long in the same village because, as a *sannyasi* (mendicant), he was forbidden from getting attached to people in the village and staying in any place permanently. He had to move on. So, early next morning, he bid goodbye to the villagers and with his bundle of possessions and his *Kamandalu* and *danda*, began his journey towards the west.

He decided to follow the course of the river in the village. The villagers had given him a warm farewell and had packed some food for him in a banana leaf. He filled his *Kamandalu* with water from the river and trudged along a path which took him near a jungle. The sun had begun to climb, and the day was getting hotter. The shimmering heat created mirages on the sand on the banks of the river and to Datta the mirages reminded him of the *Maya* (illusion) which clouded the intellect of the ignorant man. As the sun's rays became unbearably hot, he decided to rest for some time and walked into the jungle to rest under the cool shade of the trees there. He found a small patch of grass with a copse of myrtle bushes flanked by two large trees. He settled on a small rock beneath the tree and opened his lunch packet which the villagers had lovingly given him. It contained some rice with curds and a pickle to tickle his senses. He at his lunch and drank some water from his *Kamandalu*. Having finished his lunch, Datta went to the river nearby and washed his hands and face and filled his water pot with fresh water from the river and returned to his perch on the rock. He leaned against the trunk of the trees, closed his weary eyes, and dozed off.

Suddenly, he heard a loud bleating sound and awoke with a start. A few feet away in the shade of the myrtle bushes he saw a large python. It had caught a goat in its clutches and was wrapping its coils around its body squeezing it tight. The goat was bleating helplessly in deathly agony. Soon, the bleating stopped as its body was crushed by the coils of the python's body wrapped around it. The python proceeded methodically to swallow its prey slowly starting with the head of the goat. Within a period of a few minutes the goat had disappeared into the belly of the python. The python lethargically slithered under the bushes and coiled upon itself and lay quietly with its eyes half closed.

Datta watched the whole process with fascination. His mind began contemplating as to what he could learn from the python. It was a miracle of nature that a limbless creature like the python could overpower and kill a four legged creature in man's creation. Mysterious are the ways of nature, Datta said to himself. He mulled over the whole episode in his mind asking himself what he would learn from it.

* * *

The python does not go after its prey. It lies quietly in deep contemplation and accepts whatever prey comes near it. Unlike most reptiles, the python is not an active predator chasing its prey to catch it. It lies low, and whenever an animal or bird comes near it, pounces on its prey, crushes and swallows it. Once it has fed itself, it goes into a languid stupor for long periods till the next prey comes its way.

Saints are also like this. They do not run after material pursuits or food like the ordinary folk. They are confident that whatever is destined for them will reach them and they do not hanker after material possessions or gustatory satisfactions. They spend their time in silent meditation and accept what food they are given. If no food is available, they do not mind going hungry as their needs are limited. They do not waste their lives in pursuit of material sense gratification as they realize that in this life all the fruits that they receive are due to their past Karmas (<u>actions</u>*). This is called the Prarabdha Karma*. Their negative activities, if any in the past or past incarnations would bring them negative results or sorrows and all good and positive actions that they have performed in the past would translate to beneficial and positive results in this life. The saints and the wise men know that when they attribute the results of their actions to the Absolute Consciousness or Brahman, they will receive what they deserve. They understand fully well that* **they will receive what they deserve and not what they covet**. *For this is the Law of*

Karma. They clearly understand that when their minds are steadfast in the contemplation of Bhagavan (God) He will look after his needs. For it is said in the Bhagavad Gita :

अनन्याश्चिन्तयन्तो मां ये जना: पर्युपासते ।
तेषां नित्याभियुक्तानां योगक्षेमं वहाम्यहम् ॥ 9:22॥

Ananyāśh chintayanto māṁ

Yejanāḥ paryupāsate

Teṣhāṁ nityābhiyuktānāṁ

Yoga kṣhemaṁ vahāmyaham

There are those who always think of Me and engage in exclusive devotion to Me. To them, whose minds are always absorbed in Me, I provide what they lack and preserve what they already possess. [B.G. 9:22]

The saint and the wise are not inactive in the world like the resting python. But at the same time they are not actively engaged in the pursuit of pleasures and possessions of this material world. Their actions are directed to achieve spiritual refinement and not material sense gratification. To them the spiritual achievements and advancements are superior to material gains. They indulge in selfless service to help others in society and during their actions accept only what rightfully comes there way like the python.

The python, which is a limbless creature is able to overpower large four-legged creatures and subdue them. The python never for a moment thinks of its lack of limbs but depends on its powerful muscular body to overwhelm its victim. Similarly, the wise man does not think of what he lacks, but always thinks positively of what traits and skills he possesses to function in this world. One should never waste time and one's patience brooding over one's shortcomings but take advantage of one's positive skills to achieve success in this world.

The saints and the wise do not indulge in food like gourmands but control their gustatory senses and accept only the food that they are offered willingly and as alms. Food is never their priority.

* * *

Datta learnt that the saints and the wise do not hanker after food or other material possessions. They realize that they will receive what they **Deserve**. The limbless python never regrets its **Disability** but depends on its muscular body to overpower the four-legged animal. So also, the wise never regret their **Imperfections** but focus on their **Advantages**. Datta learnt from the Python the lesson of **Contentment** and to accept what life offers without complaining and cringing.

Datta's observations - Summary

PYTHON

Saints move like pythons, calm and slow,
They don't chase wants, or riches' flow.
Karma's fruits, they don't chase after,
Content with what comes, with joy and laughter.

They know the worth of seeds they sow,
Deserving they receive, that's how it'll go.
With minds on God, worries release,
He meets their needs, brings inner peace.

In saintly ways, life's path they choose,
With rhymes of virtue, they amuse.
In four-lined stanzas, truths they share,
Guiding souls through life's intricate snare.

Like limbless pythons, strong in might,
Man should rely on his own light.
Not coveting what he doesn't own,
Embrace his skills, seeds of success sown.

OCEAN

Datta decided to move on as he saw that the intensity of the sun's heat had reduced. He would have to find an appropriate place before dusk to settle down for the night. With his bundle of effects, Datta set off towards the west. He could see the river flowing to his right and he decided to follow the river. The river now seemed to flow calmly devoid of its ripples and waves. Datta surmised that the river was now approaching the ocean and hence it was calm and flowed smoothly. He continued with his onward journey. Presently, he found that the river expanded to meet the sea. The estuary was a beautiful place with trees all around, dotted with large rocks on the beach. Waves from the ocean lashed against these rocks throwing up sprays of sea water. Cormorants and other pelagic sea birds were seen in plenty and had colonized the area. Egrets and herons were fluttering about fishing in the shallow waters of the estuary. The air was filled with the squawking of sea gulls.

Datta sat on a large rock and gazed at the sea. He knew that the sea extended across the vast expanse as the **Ocean**, and both were part of the same great water body, even though semantics differentiated them geographically. The sun was rapidly descending into the ocean as if after having completed its task for the day it was rushing to take a dip in the ocean to refresh itself. Dusk was setting in. Nightfall was imminent. Datta decided to spend the night on the shores of the ocean on a large flat rocky promontory that jutted partly into the sea. The waves gently lapped against the rock producing a pleasing susurration soothing to one's ears. Datta settled down on the rock and spread his blanket. Nightfall had already set in, and the sky was festooned with twinkling stars. 'What does the ocean have to tell me', thought Datta as he contemplated on the boundless ocean that stretched before him.

"What are you thinking?", a voice beside him startled him from his reverie. He saw elderly man in a light blue robe wearing a crown of pearls.

"Who are you and what are you doing here at this late hour?", asked Datta.

"I am ***Varuna**, the God of the Seas*", said the stranger. "You are searching for knowledge, aren't you? I am here to clear your doubts about the ocean."

*   *   *

"The vast ocean which is under my control is always deep, calm, and unruffled. Only the shores of the sea show the waves which are the constant changes that occur in me. No one can fathom the depths of the ocean in which I conceal various precious gems like pearls and coral. Saints and Wise men who are storehouses of profound wisdom are also like me. Deep within their mind are hidden the gems of knowledge and wisdom. But they never flaunt their knowledge and wisdom in front of the world unless it becomes essential. The wisdom and knowledge of the saint is also unfathomable like the mighty ocean. Learn this from me."

"All the rivers of the earth flow into me. During the rainy season the rivers are often in spate and empty their waters into my bosom. So also, in summer when the sun sucks the waters to the clouds, the rivers are depleted of water and the flow into the ocean diminishes. But whatever be the situation, I maintain my level without overflowing my boundaries. I never swell up when the rains bring more water or dry up when summer dries up my feeding rivers. I maintain the same level at all times. Know this, you great Sannyasi, that all saints and wise men are like me. They maintain the same equipoise and calmness whatever situation they are in. They do not lose control of themselves and never cross the bounds of morality. Such level-headedness is a trait that the saints and I have in common. Know this from the ocean."

"The ocean is tranquil and unruffled under all circumstances like the saint who has his emotions under control and does not give in to the petty emotions that beleaguer the minds of the ignorant. The wise man is never overjoyed when he is blessed with boundless wealth or moping when he is impoverished by misfortune. He remains tranquil in all situations. This balance of mind is a state which the wise men and saints learnt from me. This is called the state of "**Sthithaprajna***."

"Know that I am formed from all the rivers and rivulets, streams and brooks, waterways, and tributaries each of which is composed of small waves and wavelets. Ultimately, know thee, that I am constituted of water particles which fill the whole ocean. So also, each living being in the universe is a part of the whole and operates as a unique individual entity which contributes to the function of the whole universe. Human beings are inherently interconnected, and the essence of existence lies in their interdependence with one another making it clear that no individual can exist in complete isolation."

"Occasionally, I am assailed by violent thunderstorms and hurricanes, but all these are only at the surface of the ocean and do not leave any permanent devastation in me. Deep down in my depths I am calm and untroubled even during the fiercest of storms. Sages and wisemen are like this. They may be pestered with criticism and scorn. On the surface they may seem disturbed by this but deep in their minds, they are never troubled by these pinpricks. They learn to convert the criticism into knowledge which encourages their advancement. Thus, they accept both praise and criticism with the same equipoise and learn to transform their critics into followers."

"As I observed earlier, all flowing water bodies enter into me, and I accept all of them without discrimination. There are contaminated waters, muddy waters, brackish waters, clean and pure water. I accept all of them with the *same enthusiasm without any prejudice. I treat all of them equally. Know thee, that the wise and the saintly are also like this. They may, in their life, encounter various types of individuals – people with external defects and internal defects. Those with* **External Defects** *of the body may be the lame, the blind, the deaf and the mute. Those with* **Internal Defects** *of the mind are the ones who do not love others, do not respect others, do not forgive others, do not have the ability to accept others, those who harbor malicious thoughts in their minds and so on. The wise and the saintly men do not reject them but learn to accept both the groups of individuals along with their defects and adjust themselves accordingly. Therein lies their greatness."*

"Once the waters reach the ocean, they merge with me and become one with me. They cannot be separated from each other. Know thee, that the wise understand this that all living forms in this world ultimately merge into the Supreme Soul which is the Brahman and there is no differentiation once they are one with the Almighty Consciousness. The bodies of individuals and all living beings are different as long as they inhabit the world, like the rivers and all other waterbodies are distinctive. But once the material body is destroyed and returned to the Panchabhootas, the Soul becomes one with the Brahman and merges with it. The wise men and the saints have realized this and hence they look upon all living beings without discrimination for **they see only the unity within them and not the morphological diversity.***"*

"The wise also realize that ultimately all the spiritual endeavors are to achieve this state of merger with the Brahman, which is called Moksha. Hence, they understand that whichever religious path one takes, it all ultimately leads to the same Universal Truth or Consciousness. They

have succinctly capsulized this into a verse which runs thus emphasizing **the Universality of All Religions.**

आकाशात् पतितं तोयं यथा गच्छति सागरम् ।
सर्वदेवनमस्कारः केशवं प्रति गच्छति ॥

**Aakashath Pathitham Thoyam,
Yatha Gachathi Sagaram
Sarvadeva Namaskaram,
Keshavam Prathi Gachathi**

As the water that falls down as rain from the sky finally reaches the Ocean, the worship of any divine aspect ultimately reaches the Supreme Being.

Thus, as the rivers and rain merge into oneness into me, all prayers in the world lead to the same God which can be called by many names.

एकं सद् विप्रा बहुधा वदन्ति
Ekam Sad Vipra Bahudha Vadanti.

"The Truth is One, people call it by different names.*" This eternal truth is realized by the sages and wise men who practice it in every walk of life and appreciate the oneness of all living beings among the diversity in the Universe."*

* * *

The ocean thus taught Datta the need to maintain **Equipoise** in all emotional situations and recognize the **Oneness of the Universe** even among its diversity. The Wise are a treasury of **Profound Wisdom** like the pearls and corals in the ocean depths. Saints and the Wise learn to be **Level-headed** and never cross the bounds of **Morality**. All the waters in the Universe are part of the same entity. So also, all Living Beings in the World are **Interconnected** and **Interdependent**. As all waters ultimately reach the Ocean, all **Souls** ultimately merge with the **Supreme Soul** or **Brahman**. The Saints and the Wise see only the **Unity of the Souls** and not the **Morphological Diversity**.

The sun had already risen when Datta woke up to the squawking of the sea gulls and cormorants. He bundled up his belongings and made his way towards the mouth of the river to have his bath and daily ablutions. Once he had completed this, he sat in the shade of a tree and performed his daily *Japa** (chanting) and meditation. He decided to move south where he was told there was a large town where the king's palace stood. He trudged towards south following a beaten path through the jungle.

Datta's observations - Summary

OCEAN

In depths so dark, the ocean lies,
Concealing treasures from prying eyes.
Wisemen hold knowledge, a treasury's keep,
Yet humbly they guard their wisdom's sweep.

Rivers may flood, and summers, parch,
Yet the ocean's boundary remains steadfast arch.
So, too, the wise, in equipoise dwell,
Morality's bounds, they'll never quell.

In storms, the surface churns in fear,
But deep within, a calm premiere.
The saints and wise, a mirrored reflection,
Balanced and serene, they weather affliction.

All waters flow, their paths converge,
Embraced by the ocean, no soul shall diverge.
Just like saints, with love so pure,
They embrace all, in kindness endure.

All waters merge, become the one,
Ocean's embrace, their journey's done.
Souls unite, in cosmic blend,
Brahman's love, their final end.

One Truth, diverse in its names,
In unity, all life proclaims.
The wise and saintly comprehend,
Love's the force, that'll never bend.

MOTH

For the next two hours, Datta was focused on moving south towards the seaside town. As he neared the town, he could see people busily moving around. The paths were wide, and the roads had been paved with cobblestones. Horses and horse drawn carriages were moving about on the roads. On either side of the road, he found lean-tos where traders were busy peddling their wares. There were shops selling clothes, grocery, vegetables, and fruit. Pots and pans of various sizes and shapes hung from hooks in front of the shops. Some of the shops sported leather goods and teenage boys were hawking their wares of lamps and shades. Datta walked along the street admiring the wares and the merchandise till he reached the street corner where a temple frequented by the town folk stood. He washed his feet in the small temple pond and went inside the temple for a *darshan* (vision) of the deity. The idol was that of *Shiva*, one of the trinity of Hindu Gods. He prostrated before the *sanctum sanctorum** and sat in a corner of the mandapam and recited the *Rudram* and *Chamakum* (prayers to Shiva). He sat in meditation for some time. He had been out of his father's *Ashramam* for almost two months now. Only half of his journey of seeking knowledge from *Nature* was over. He had another two months before would return to the *Ashramam* of Sage Atri.

As he was pondering over the future course of action, the priest, who had completed the afternoon *Pooja* (worship) approached him with folded hands.

"Swamiji, I am pleased to welcome you to this temple of *Bhagavan Mahadeva* (another name of *Shiva*). You seem to be new to these parts. I have not seen you here before."

The priest was an elderly man with a tonsured head and a *shikha* (long tuft of hair) at the back of his head. On his forehead, he sported the three horizontal lines of *Vibhuthi* (sacred ash) which is the hallmark of the followers of *Bhagavan Shiva*.

"Datta respectfully folded his hands and identified himself. "My name is Datta. I am the son and *sishya* of Sage Atri and come from his *Ashramam*. I am in search of knowledge from *Nature* and so far during the last two months have learnt many things. I have to travel and gather more knowledge from *Nature*."

"I would be honored if you could stay with us in our home. My wife and I will be greatly pleased to receive you as our *Athithi* (guest)."

Datta did not reply immediately. He began, "I am a *Sannyasi* and hence do not stay in *grihas* (homes) permanently. I shall be pleased to be your guest for tonight. But tomorrow onwards, for a few days, permit me to spend my time in the *mandapam* in this temple. I could partake of the *Prasadam* (offering to God) from the temple, for my needs are few."

"So be it", agreed the priest. You may accompany me when I go home after the temple is closed after the evening *Pooja* today. You can share with me whatever you have learnt from your travel and thus enlighten me with your wisdom and knowledge."

The priest led Datta to his home. It was a small house which was part of the *Agraharam* (row of houses near a temple). Outside the house was a small corridor open to the street. The priest's wife was a petite elderly lady with greying hair and *Kumkumam* (tilak) on her forehead. A string of jasmine flowers adorned her hair and spread fragrance all around the house. She welcomed Datta and brought him water to wash his feet before entering the house. Datta and the priest sat on straw mats on the floor and the priest's wife served them soft *iddlis* (steamed rice cakes) and plantains on a banana leaf. A tumbler of warm milk was offered to Datta and the priest.

After eating the frugal dinner, Datta and the priest sat on the corridor outside the house and discussed various subjects on spirituality and philosophy. Datta gave him a synopsis of his journey and the wisdom that he had gathered from *Nature* during the travels. As it was nearing midnight, Datta offered to lie down in the corridor and the priest retired into the house for the night leaving a burning oil lamp in the corridor.

Datta lay down thinking of his plans for the next day. It had rained in the evening and the air was replete with moths and crane flies circling the flame of the oil lamp which stood in a corner. As he was watching, Datta saw a couple of moths fly into the fire and get burnt. Some crane flies also, attracted by the bright flame of the burning oil lamp plunged into the fire only to be singed and killed. Moths that plunged into the fire had their wings singed and fell to the floor where they were attacked by fiery ants which dragged them to the ant hill nearby. Thus, attracted by the bright flame of the oil lamp, the moths and crane flies met their miserable end. This got Datta thinking on the fate of the unfortunate moths.

* * *

*It was the **sense of Sight** that had led to the death of these insects. The bright flame had lured them to their disaster. Often man is also hoodwinked into disaster with his eyes. Seeing the voluptuous body of women, men may be* attracted to them, little knowing that they may end up ruining their reputation and themselves. The pleasant thought of the anticipation of sex lures many a man to the lustful embrace of a woman and this may prove catastrophic for him. He may be led into disaster and ruin inadvertently owing to his lust and desire for carnal gratification. Many a man falls into such a honey trap. For a moment he forgets the teachings of his Gurus and his masters and the moral lessons that he learnt are shrouded in Maya as he falls prey to the cravings of sense gratification.

Not only Women and sex, but humans are attracted by Wealth, Jewelry and Apparel which are another cause for their downfall like the unfortunate moth. Instead of attaching his mind to these material possessions and ephemeral distractions, man should learn to yoke his mind to the Supreme Being or Brahman and thereby strive to attain Moksha which should be the aim of every human being. Enticed by the illusory pleasures of the senses, man gets caught in this cycle of Samsara – of birth and death.

The moth that flew to its death lured by the brightness of the flame made Datta realize how the **Sense of Sight** could lead one to disaster. Man is often lured by **Lust and Love** into relationships which may prove detrimental to his reputation and himself. **Saints** and **the** Wise avoid these ephemeral material attractions of the world and fix their minds on the **Supreme Brahman** which leads them to **Moksha**. The moth taught Datta how the sense of sight can be mislead one to disaster.

Datta's observations   -   Summary

MOTH

In shadows danced, the moth's cruel plight,
Lured by the flame, its sense of sight.
As man, too, falls to pleasures' lure,
And meets disaster, heart impure.

Desire's embrace, a tempting woe,
To lust's abyss, his soul may go.
With gold and wealth, a path misled,
To downfall's door where dreams are dead.

Yet, saints and sages, pure of heart,
Seek Brahman's truth, to Moksha's start.
Their minds and sights set on the One,
In blissful grace, their souls are spun.

BEE

Datta was up early morning the next day, and after his bath and daily *Japa* bid farewell to the priest and his wife thanking them profusely for their hospitality. He walked towards the temple to partake in the *Pooja* in the temple. He sat for a while in the temple *mandapam* when many devotees came to him for blessings and spiritual advice. They bowed before him and offered him fruit and flowers. Datta remained in the temple till noon. In the evening he decided to visit the royal garden of the king which was open to public.

He ambled towards the garden and found a large shady tree in the center of the garden. There was a platform around the tree built with boulders from the riverbed. Datta seated himself comfortably on the platform observing the happenings in the garden. Near him was a bush of sweet smelling flowers of various types and colors. On his right was a small pond with a luxuriant growth of lotus blooms. Beetles, butterflies, and wasps were buzzing around these aromatic flowers and sucking nectar from them. Bumble bees and honeybees were seen in plenty and Datta could see a honeycomb high in the branches of the tree where he was sitting.

The sight of the flowers and bees sucking nectar from the flowers set Datta's mind thinking. "What could these tiny creatures of God teach me?", he wondered. Every creation of God in this world has a purpose in life. Every little creature, every little plant or tree has something new to teach us. These little flying insects also form an important part of the ecosystem in God's creation. They too must have something to contribute and teach me", thought Datta. This set him reflecting.

* * *

Bumble bees and honeybees buzzed around the flowers and very gently alighted on them without hurting or damaging the flowers. With their long proboscis, they imperceptibly sucked the nectar from the flowers. The insects remained in the flower for only a very short while and flitted to the next flower to repeat the process.

A sannyasi, mused, Datta should be like the bees. He should receive only very little food as alms and partake of the food that he has taken from the homes of the Grihastha*. For the sannyasi, his hand is his plate, and his stomach is the vessel in which he stores the food. He does not hoard food for the next meal. The bumble bee does not save the nectar that it sucks but takes only the little amount needed to fulfil its hunger. So should be the wise and the saintly. The food consumed by them should be limited in quantity, just enough for their needs.

The saint and the wise should never resort to excess eating. Excess food always dulls the senses and renders one torpid. Excess feeding renders the intellect sluggish and retards the learning process. Hence like the bumble bee, the wise should learn to limit their food intake to keep body and soul together and not give in to gastronomic indulgence.

A king or a ruler should also be like the bumble bee. He should take taxes from his subjects without causing grief to them. Taxes should be collected by the king from his subjects depending on the availability of funds leaving them satisfied but not impoverished. In return, the king should also give his subjects a good regime where all the needs of the populace are fulfilled. The bumble bee which takes the nectar out of the flower, helps pollinate the flower to help the fruits develop. But the bees do not partake of the fruit which they help to generate. This is indeed a marvel in Nature's masterplan. Thus, the bees and the flowers formed a partnership each one helping the other in one way or the other. Just like the bee sucks out the nectar without harming the flowers, man should learn to do his duty in society with diligence without hurting anyone in his line of duty. Man should learn this from the bees, mused, Datta.

One bumble bee which hovered too long on the lotus flower in the pond met with disaster. The bee had spent too much time in the flower sucking the nectar and when the sun went down, the petals of the flower closed, and the bee was trapped within the flower and met its end. Similarly, Datta reflected, the saint or a guest should never overstay his welcome in the same place, lest he meet with despair. A sannyasi should never stay in the same household or receive alms from them repeatedly, as this can lead to attachment and be a source of remorse.

The honeybees on the other hand, unlike the bumblebee, gathered the nectar from the flowers and carried it to the beehive to be stored. So also, thought Datta, a wise man should learn widely from the scriptures, but assimilate only the essence of the scriptures. Even though he may be widely read, it is imperative that he memorize and retain only the quintessence of the teachings and use them for the benefit of others.

At the same time, Datta felt that the honeybee which was hoarding the honey in the beehive was not wise enough. For the honey thus stored is often stolen by the honey gatherer who steals the honey from the beehive and thus deprives the bees of their stored honey. Wise men also thus do not hoard wealth which could form an inducement for thieves to steal their possessions. The wealth of the wise men should be put to good use for the benefit of society. The saints thus do not accumulate wealth as this would lead to attachments developing thus leading them astray from the spiritual path which they pursue. They should understand that material possessions are of no use when finally death overtakes the body. One has to leave the body behind along with all his possessions as only the Soul can reach the astral planes.

Datta saw the beehive where the bees buzzed around the hive and helped each other. He realized the advantage of community living from the bees. The honey gathered by the bees was for the whole community and not for the individual bee which brought the honey to the hive. From them, Datta realized the importance of **Cooperation**. In a group or community everyone cannot think or act alike. A community is always formed of different types of people with different characters and attitudes. So, difference of opinion will always occur in a group. Whatever be the differences, if the common aim or goal of the group is understood by everyone and if they are ready to cooperate to work towards that goal, the group will be cohesive and successful. It is like the fingers in one's hand. Each finger is different, but together they can achieve wonders. But the individual fingers cannot act alone to achieve great things. The bees made Datta realize the advantage of working in a group, co-operating with the other members in the community so that progress and success will be faster for the whole community.

The honeybee taught him a lesson on **Perseverance**. Whatever happens to the honeycomb and even if all the collected honey is lost, the honeybee does not lose heart. It never stops working or sits sulking. It goes around as usual gathering honey from flowers and starts a fresh cycle of honey gathering. This persevering nature of the honeybee warrants imitation by a man of wisdom. Man should develop the mindset to persist in life however adverse be the circumstances. He should let go off the past misfortunes and march forward with single minded determination to achieve his goal. If so, he will never taste failure. He should persevere towards his goal. **An aim without perseverance or perseverance without an aim is a sure recipe for failure.**

At the same time another thought struck Datta. It was a negative thought about the honeybee. The honeybee stored the honey that it collected diligently in its honeycomb. But alas, the honey-gatherer seeing the large honeycomb on the branch of the tree, destroyed the comb and stole the honey that the bees had so laboriously collected and stored. Likewise, Datta realized that the saintly and the wise do not hoard food or wealth for there is ample opportunity for *swindlers and crooks to relieve them of their hoarded possessions. A fool and his wealth are thus soon parted, realized Datta.*

* * *

These thoughts flashed through Datta's mind as he keenly observed the bumble bees and the honeybees buzzing around the flowers in the arbor. **Persistence** in one's duty, **Not Hurting** others in one's line of duty, **Not Hoarding** wealth, **Community Living, Co-operation,** and **Mutual Benefit** to others were the lessons Datta learnt from the bumble bee and the honeybee. The Wise should accept from society only the **Minimal Amount** of food that they need.

Datta's observations - Summary

BEE

In gardens where the flowers bloom,
The bee alights, a gentle groom.
Sipping nectar, a tiny share,
Without harm, it does not impair.

Like saints who eat with grace so light,
To nourish, but not gluttonous might.
A king must tax with thoughtful care,
And rule with kindness, just and fair.

The bee, a pollinator's role,
No fruit it takes to reach its goal.
Like saints who do not overstay,
In harmony, they find their way.

The essence of the scriptures sought,
By saints who learn, but hoard nought.
Yet, thieves may come for hoarded gold,
Like hunters who seek treasures old.

Bees unite, their strength they share,
Like fingers joined, they do declare.
Cooperate, in harmony stand,
Together, making a stronger band.

Though hives destroyed, they'll still persist,
Perseverance, a bee's true gist.
Learn from them, do not despair,
With tenacity, life we bear.

ELEPHANT

As is his wont, Datta did not stay in the town for long. He bade farewell to the priest and his wife thanking them for their hospitality and proceeded south towards the next village. The priest told him that his path would go through the jungle where often there were mahouts who camped to capture elephants. The jungle was not usually populated by wild animals though herbivores like deer and bison were not uncommon. The priest's wife packed him a lunch of cooked lemon rice with pickles neatly wrapped in a banana leaf and some curd in a small earthen pot. He filled his *Kamandalu* with water from the priest's well and set off towards the edge of the town along the path that led him through the jungle.

For the next two hours he made his way through the jungle following the path which the priest had mapped for him. By noon it was hot and he reached a clearing and decided to take rest in the shade of a tree. Weary from his travel, he sat down to relish the food given to him by the priest's wife. He ate the lemon rice, drank the curd, and washed his hands in a nearby pool. He sat under the tree, leaned against the trunk and closed his eyes.

The loud trumpeting of an elephant woke him up from his slumber. He looked around. In the distance, he could hear loud voices of people shouting and elephants trumpeting. He remembered that the priest had told him that there was a *Khedda* (a place where elephants are trapped) in the jungle. He walked towards the area where the sound emanated from. Soon he reached a clearing where there were a group of mahouts who were engaged in restraining a trapped elephant.

A female elephant had been used to lure the wild male elephants into the ditch which was palisaded by tall logs of wood made into an enclosure surrounded by a moat. Once the wild bull elephants entered the enclosure, the gate was closed. Thus, the elephants were trapped in the enclosure. With the help of trained elephants called *Kumkis*, the captured wild elephants were then tamed and domesticated. This was the procedure employed in the capture of the wild elephants. After watching the whole procedure for a while, Datta returned to the clearing where he sat under the tree contemplating what he saw.

The bull-elephant is lured into the pit prepared for the capture by a trained cow-elephant. When the bull-elephant enters the pit sensing the presence of the female elephant through the keen sense of smell, the cow-elephant erotically rubs against the body of the bull-elephant, thus stimulating it sensually. This provocative caress of the cow-elephant charms the male into subjugation. In this enamored state, the bull-elephant is captured and its legs chained by the mahouts.

* * *

Datta sat thinking of the captured elephant. The bull-elephant is ensnared into captivity by the **Sense of Touch** of the female elephant. When the female elephant rubs against the body of the male caressing it, the lust provoked in the bull-elephant inebriates its mind to fall for the enticement of the female leading to its capture.

Man also often falls into this honeytrap of lust and passion which leads him towards disaster. Man too is bound by the chains of infatuation for the female and often loses his sense of discrimination and acuity which can lead to his downfall. Passionate persons tempted by the opposite gender may fall into this honeytrap and meet with disaster.

When elephants move in herds, often the male elephants which try to mate with a female have to face the wrath of other bull-elephants in the herd. Often a fight ensues, and suitor often gets injured or even killed. This is true in the case of humans also. Crimes of passion are well known in case of humans. Enticed by the opposite sex, man often gets into trouble or disaster when he encounters fondling by the opposite sex. The wise and the saintly are hence careful to avoid these pitfalls in life. History bears ample proof for such incidents.

Love is an emotion that should open one's eyes. It is an emotion that a person feels towards another in this life. But if love makes a person blind, then one should realize that it is not true love. Such a love may be called selfish love or lust. When one feels love and it makes him think only of himself and not of others, it is certain that love has made him blind. If he forgets the path that he has travelled this far when he is in love, it means that he has been blinded by love. If his love for someone turns into hate towards others, it indicates that he is overcome by blind love. *If love makes him digress from the path of Dharma or truth, it is blind love. Love that turns him against his close kith and kin is also blind.*

All these need to be considered when one falls in love. One has to understand whether the love opens his eyes towards the truth or makes him close his eyes towards the realities of life. Love which opens his eyes, will give him happiness in his future. But if love blinds him, then that love gives him temporary, transient happiness at the present moment, but later on it will give him unhappiness and sorrow. So, when in love such a self-analysis becomes important.

* * *

Thus, realized Datta, the elephant was lured into its downfall by its **Sense of Touch** and **Lust** for the opposite sex. Man often falls prey to **Sensuality** and **Infatuation** towards the opposite sex which leads to his downfall. **Passion** often leads man to misery. Datta realized that **Blind Love** which is against the principles of **Dharma** often leads to disaster.

The mahouts near the *Khedda* invited Datta to spend the night with them in the camp. They respectfully offered Datta fruits and coconut water which he gratefully accepted. He set up camp in the clearing under a tree and went to sleep with the stars twinkling overhead and the moon dousing the whole forest with its silvery light. He had a hard journey ahead of him through the forest the next day.

Datta's observations   -   Summary

ELEPHANT

In nature's dance, the touch does spark,
A lust that lures the male's embrace.
Yet heedless passion leaves a mark,
As man succumbs to tragic grace.

In rivalry, they clash and fight,
Like elephants that quake the ground.
Love's blindness takes them from the light,
Selfish desire, their hearts are bound.

But saints and sages, wise and clear,
Know well the perils lust can breed.
In selfishness, they steer with cheer,
And from this treacherous path, they heed.

For in the morass, dangers lie,
A path to certain, dire dismay.
To rise above, their spirits fly,
In wisdom's arms, they safely stay.

DEER

Datta woke up early as usual and went for a dip in the nearby river. The sun was peeping over the horizon when he began his journey through the forest after bidding farewell to the group of mahouts who were busy tying chains to the feet of the elephants that had been trapped the day before. Datta picked up his belongings and followed the path which would take him out of the forest towards the next village. The mahouts had given him instructions on how to reach the next village and accordingly he set forth following their directive.

As he walked through the forest with its dense cluster of trees and bushes and the overhanging wines, he found that the forest was becoming thicker and darker. The overhead sun was obscured by the branches and the thick foliage. His movement had become slow as the path was slowly winding uphill, and he was moving up a small hillock that had to be crossed before he reached the village which was on the opposite side of the hill. Presently he came to the top of the hill and beyond the hill he could see a valley with the village far away. He began descending the hill and soon reached the foot of the hill. The forest had become less dense, and the trees were few and far apart. He came upon a large stretch of grassland which extended up to the banks of the river beyond.

Datta found a convenient spot under the shade of a tree and sat down to catch his breath. The mahouts had given him a couple of flat breads made of wheat with a little vegetable curry which he ate. He leaned against the tree and closed his eyes. A little far from where he sat he saw a herd of deer grazing in the field. There were both bucks and does. A couple of fawns were prancing about the field. Datta sat admiring those beautiful creatures with their spotted golden brown coats as they majestically browsed in the field. Occasionally a buck with exquisitely branching horns would look up as if it had heard a predator in the bushes, prick its ears and on finding no hidden danger, would continue to nibble at the grass.

One of the females, a young doe seemed to prick its ears at some noise and focus its eyes on the spot in the forest where the noise was coming from. It was the sound of a flute. The divine melody of the flute reminded Datta of the transcendental melody of *Bhagavan Sri Krishna's* flute which attracted the Gopis to his presence. The ethereal soft melody emanating from the flute was bewitching to the senses. For a moment Datta was also entranced by the melodious refrain. Slowly, the doe began to stroll towards the sound as if bewitched. The music was so alluring that Datta himself felt mesmerized by it. Meanwhile the doe was approaching the edge of the forest, and the music appeared to come from a copse of trees. The doe approached the trees.

All of a sudden, a large net dropped down from one of the trees and the doe was snared in the net. It struggled to free itself, but the more it struggled, the more it was entangled in the net. Soon two men scrambled down from the trees and caught the struggling doe. They were poachers who had set the trap to snare the doe. They tied the legs of the doe together and carried it away on a pole. Datta shuddered at the thought of what would happen to the poor doe. It would be sold in the market. May be someone would buy it for its tasty venison meat, or another could own it for the beautiful deerskin leather used to make goods or if luck would have it a young maiden or princess could buy it to be reared as a pet in her palace.

* * *

It was the **Sense of Hearing** *that had proven calamitous for the poor deer. Deer are attracted by sweet melodies and music and the poachers take advantage of this fact to trap the deer.*

Likewise, Datta reflected, saints and wise men should avoid falling prey to sweet melodies, musical entertainments and singing which can distract them from their single mindedness in the pursuit of knowledge and wisdom. The wise man should learn this from the deer that music and dance are distractions that can bewilder the intellect and distract one's mind away from the ultimate goal which he is seeking in life.

A Brahmachari (<u>student</u>*) should also be aware of this and not fritter away his precious years which should be devoted only to study and acquiring knowledge. He should avoid unwanted gossip and slandering conversation which would definitely distract him from his focused goal in life. A student also should be vary of such distractions that can divert attention away from his studies.*

Whatever be one's goal in life, one should not give in to the distraction of the sense organs to deviate from one's chosen path in life.

The story of sage Rishyasringa* bears ample testimony to the fact that man can be lured by the sweet melodies of music and can forget his duties and Karmas in life.

A spiritual aspirant can easily be bogged down by passions and sensual desires and thus lose sight of his transcendental journey towards the truth. So also, even wise men, if they fall victim to praise and sycophantic flattery can digress from their path towards success and bring about their own downfall. Men, spellbound by such flattery could be misled into disaster. This was the lesson that Datta learnt from the incident of the deer. One should not be misled by one **sense of hearing**.

Datta realized that the deer was tricked by the poachers into a trap. Just so, in life, if a person is cheated or defrauded by a person, he should learn a lesson from it. But if the person is being deceived repeatedly by the same person, the fault may not be in the deceiver but in the victim. The victim should learn that the decisions that he is making are wrong. All the people in the world are not good and straightforward. It is the straightforward and the honest man who gets deceived easily. **In a forest full of trees, the trees which stand erect and tall are always cut first.**

*   *   *

Datta realized that of the five sense organs, it was the **Sense of Hearing** that was the reason for the ruination of the deer. Man also is led astray by **Music** and **Entertainment** if he does not exercise caution in its indulgence. Listening to **Praise** and **Sycophantic Flattery** can lead to man's downfall. One must be careful what one **Hears** and **Listens to**. **Gossip** and **Slander** should not divert the **Brahmachari** from his main goal in life.

Datta's observations - Summary

DEER

In woods where shadows dance and play,
The poachers' music lures its prey.
A sweet, melodious, siren's call,
Entraps the deer, they soon enthrall.

The saints and sages, wisdom sought,
Shun tempting tunes, distraction fought.
For in pursuit of truths divine,
They silence songs, their souls align.

The *Brahmachari*, pure in heart,
Must guard his mind, a sacred art.
From gossip's snare and slander's sting,
His studies soar, knowledge he'll bring.

Beware the flattery's honeyed snare,
It veils the truth, blinds with glare.
To focus on the one Supreme,
The *Brahman's* grace, life's dearest dream.

FISH

The heat had subsided even though the sun was still high above the horizon. Datta began walking carrying his meagre possessions. He decided to follow the river as he was sure that this would lead him to the next town which was quite large and was named *Videha*. He decided to quicken his pace as he wanted to reach the village before sunset. After an hour's journey, he sat down to rest on a log of wood which he found on the banks of the river. He went to the river, washed himself, and quenched his thirst. As he was returning, he noticed a couple of fishermen coming to the river. They had long poles with them with a fishing line and hooks at the end of the line. The hooks contained a piece of flesh which they used as bait for the fish. To attract the fish, they initially sprinkled some puffed rice on the water. Immediately a shoal of fish appeared and began thrashing about to feed on the grains that were scattered in the water. There were fishes of all sizes and types. When the fish were feeding on the rice, the anglers cast their lines into their midst and waited. Soon the fish swallowed the bait, and the anglers pulled out the line and caught the fish. Fishes of various sizes and type were easily caught by them using pieces of meat and worms as their bait. Datta watched this for a while and returned to his seat and sat on the log of wood mulling over what he had just seen.

The fish had succumbed to the baited hook of the anglers lured by its **Sense of Taste**. The fish, unaware of the fisherman's ruse swallowed the tasty morsel speared on to the hook and thus sealed their own fate. This set Datta thinking.

*   *   *

Man, too often betrayed by his gustatory sense, seeks his own ruin. He is unable to control his tongue, and the sense of taste often leads him to disaster. Food is a great allure for man, and he is often unable to resist the temptation to gobble up rich food which tickles his palate. He forgets that he has to eat to live and not live to eat. The most difficult sense to control is one of taste and the person who controls his sense of taste is able to control his other senses easily. Unless the tongue is conquered, mastery over the other senses cannot be achieved. Man should realize that the material pleasures of the world are the hook of Maya which will bait him and lead him towards his downfall. The fish thus teaches man to let go off greed and gluttony.

When a person fasts, all his four other senses get subdued, but the sense of taste become sharper when he is fasting, and the appetite becomes more intense. The other senses may be dulled into inactivity while fasting, but not the tongue which may in turn seek more gustatory pleasures. Hence, the wise and the saintly learn to control their tongue and be abstemious in their eating habits.

Their food is mainly the Prasadam that has been offered to God. They keep their sense of taste under control and avoid the spicy and appetizing food and partake of bland food only to keep their bodies functioning.

Another important function of the tongue is its role in **Communication***. When a saint or a wise man controls his tongue, he is guarded about his conversation. He is very careful to keep his conversation Saatvic (*righteous*), not resorting to lies, harsh words or words that hurt others. The saint's words are always spent in singing the praise of the Supreme Being just as his mind is spent in His contemplation. Softly spoken, sweet words of wisdom are the attributes of a man of wisdom. Speaking ill of others, gossip, calumny, and hypocrisy are alien to his character.*

It is man's desire for sensual pleasures that drive him towards his doom like the greedy fish which is attracted by the morsels of food that the angler scatters before baiting the fish. Man also often meets his doom when he runs in search of material pleasures of life losing sight of his own greatness.

The fish never leaves the water which is its home. Similarly, the wise man never loses sight of his true self and does not waver from the fact that he is the soul which is part of the Supreme Being. The wise realize that they are spiritual beings (souls) clothed in a human body.

Another lesson which the fish teaches us is to swim against the stream. Whatever be the force of the water and however strong the flow of the river, the fish happily swims upstream along the river to reach its destination. The flow of the river does not retard its progress. Similarly, the wise men are able to achieve their goals with single minded focus whatever be the odds against them achieving success. They are like the fish that swim against the strong currents in the river.

* * *

Datta came out of his reverie. He was surprised by the amount of information that the fish could teach him, though in a negative manner. The **Sense of Taste** proved deadly for the fish. Man who is unable to curb his tongue often finds it deleterious to his health. **Greed** and **Gluttony** can lead to a calamitous outcome. Abuse of one's tongue in **Communication** proves disastrous to those who are not cautious. Saints and the Wise realize this and curb their tongue. The fish taught Datta that man should **Face all Odds** and swim against the current in the river of life to be successful in his endeavors.

Datta stood up and trudged along the path towards the city of *Videha* where he intended to spend his night that day. He could see the city far away with its large buildings and their turrets. Some of the buildings were large with domes crowning them. Far away Datta saw the gleaming palace of the king which stood majestically at the center of the city surrounded by large ramparts. Quickening his pace, he hastened towards the city.

Datta's observations - Summary

FISH

In waters deep, the fish's greed entwines,
To tasty bait, he heedlessly inclines.
Hooked to his death, a tale of woe is spun,
As allure leads to man's disaster won.

But saints and sages, wise in virtue's art,
Control their senses, mastering their heart.
To eat for life, not live to eat alone,
They find the path to peace and be well-known.

Maya's delight, material pleasures snare,
A perilous path that leads to despair.
Yet wise ones learn to let go of despair,
Their spirits soar, released from earthly mire.

Sweet-spoken words from saintly tongues arise,
No falsehoods mar the truth within their eyes.
With tender hearts, they lift others above,
No words of hurt, but boundless wells of love.

As fish find home in waters they reside,
The wise know the *Atman's* their true guide.
Their soul's abode, beyond life's fleeting foam,
They dwell in peace and never feel alone.

Against the currents, fish swim undeterred,
Their strength and grace in harmony conferred.
So too, wise souls face life's relentless tide,
And swim against odds with courage as their guide.

PINGALA the COURTESAN

Datta arrived at the outskirts of the city of *Videha*. It was a large city with wide roads and shops on either side. At the center of the city stood the king's palace, a large structure surrounded by a large fortress. On either side of the citadel stood rows of large houses, probably the houses of the chieftains and other members of the king's court. Datta walked along the street looking at these with wonder. This was the first time that he was visiting such a large city. The streets were crowded with horse-drawn carriages and horsemen trotting along. A stray bullock cart carrying wares to the market was seen rambling along the street. Mounted soldiers armed with swords were patrolling the streets. The whole city reeked of opulence.

Datta crossed the center of the city and reached a quieter part of the city. Here, the houses were few and far apart. He trudged along the road not knowing where to spend the night as dusk was setting in already. An old woman stooped over with age was walking along the road using a cane for support. She carried a heavy bag in her hand and was finding it difficult to see her way in the twilight. She stumbled and was about to fall, when Datta held her by the arm and steadied her. The old woman looked up at Datta with grateful eyes.

"Who are you O! Sannyasi, you seem to be a stranger to this city."

"Yes, *Amma* (mother), Datta replied folding his hands respectfully. I am coming from far away and am a *Brahmachari* travelling the country to gain knowledge and experience. I just now came into this large city, and I am at a loss to find out a place to stay for the night. Is there a temple or a *Satram* nearby where I can rest for the night?"

The old woman looked him up shading her eyes with her hands, "Oh! young man, you are at the wrong end of the city. The temple and the *Satram* are at the other end of this city and is a bit far from here. You may not be able to find it in the dark. This part of the city is err....not a good neighborhood for the pious types like you." she replied with a cackle. "But nevertheless, I will help you. My house is nearby. I stay there with my granddaughter, Pingala. She works at the king's palace during daytime. My house is large enough for you to stay. There is a small cottage annexed to my home where you can rest for the night. It is empty now. In the morning I will direct you to the temple."

Datta agreed and accompanied the woman. He helped carry the heavy bag for her. On the way she said, "My granddaughter may not approve of my decision to shelter you for the night, but don't give heed to her words. I will talk to her."

Datta followed her silently. Presently they came to a large bungalow with a tiled roof, one and a half stories, a widely bracketed gable roof and a veranda running all around the house. Nearby stood a small single-room cottage with a small veranda in front.

"You can stay there," said the old woman pointing to the cottage. "There is only one room inside. I will bring some fruits and a bowl of milk for you." So saying, she took her bag from Datta and went into the large bungalow.

Soon, she came with a platter of fruits and a bowl of warm cow's milk and placed it before Datta. Datta had meanwhile washed his face, hands and feet and unpacked his bundle. He felt very hungry, and the platter of fruit seemed appetizing. "You can sleep in the cottage. Don't be bothered if you hear any noises at night, for my granddaughter, Pingala goes to bed very late at night. We may have visitors later in the night. I will leave this lighted oil lamp here for you."

Only then, did it dawn on Datta that this was probably the home of a courtesan, a house of ill repute. Paramours could visit her at night and perhaps that was what the old woman had indirectly warned him about. Datta being beyond these emotions, decided to ignore this and retire for the night. After his dinner, he decided to sleep outside on the veranda as it was cooler outside. He spread his sheet on the veranda and using his bundle as a head rest, lay down to sleep. As he lay, he began thinking of his adventures during the day and was ruminating on them and formulating verses to be composed the next day.

He heard the door of the bungalow open. Datta raised his head and saw a beautiful woman decked in elegant jewelry standing at the door leaning against the doorframe. She wore a beautiful sari of light pink shade with a matching blouse. Her hair was plaited and decked with a string of jasmine flowers which spread its fragrance all around. Her lips were stained red with the betel leaves and areca nut which she was chewing. Her eyes were lined with kohl and a large red *bindi* adorned her forehead. 'This must be Pingala', thought Datta.

It was obvious that she was a courtesan awaiting the arrival of her concubine. The woman seemed restless. She waited at the door for a while and then went inside only to return to the door and watch the road on either side of the house as if eagerly waiting for the arrival of someone. As time passed, she seemed to become frustrated and began wringing her hands in despair. For, the person whom she expected did not seem turn up to visit her.

A few men passed by the house, but no one even glanced in her direction. They ignored her. A horse drawn carriage with a rich aristocratic nobleman rolled by but did not stop at her doorstep. Her countenance blossomed with hope each time a carriage passed by but clouded with despair when she was ignored. Hoping that someone wealthy would come to offer her enough riches or a generous gift today, she continued to stand at the doorstep with her eyes glued to the street.

Watching her, Datta felt a mixed emotion of pity and remorse. He mentally blessed her and said a prayer to the *Bhagavan Sri Krishna* to relieve her of her distress just as he had helped the crippled woman *Kubja** when he visited *Mathura*. The night wore on and the woman seemed to get more restive.

Suddenly, a change seemed to come over her. So far she had been standing slouched against the doorpost overwhelmed with disappointment and frustration. Suddenly she straightened. A strange transformation seemed to occur in her. Datta watched in wonderment. A feeling of *Vairagya* (<u>austere detachment</u>) seemed to overcome her.

She plucked the string of flowers from her hair and flung it onto the street and went inside and shut the door with a bang as if closing the doors to her past. Through the open window, Datta saw her remove all her jewelry and hurl them onto the couch in the room. See sat on the couch and buried her face in her hands. A sob rose from her throat and broke out into a full throated wail. She remained whimpering for a while. Then suddenly, she stood up and went to the corner of the room where a *tambura* (stringed musical instrument) stood against the wall. With single pointed resoluteness, she began plucking the strings of the *tambura* and burst into a song. The heart-rending lyrics of the song ran thus:

In the realm of my illusion's sway,
My mind, untamed, led me astray
Yearning for pleasures, sinful and gray
From men enslaved, their desires betray

Oh, the suffering I have brought upon me
Selling my body, a painful decree,
For pleasures fleeting, how could I not see,
This vessel mere excrement, will never be free?

For this body of skin, hair, and nails,
Releasing foul substances, as nature prevails,
Temporary pleasures, illusion unveils,
Why did I hope in them, my spirit trails?

Bhagavan Vishnu's mercy, a mystery untold,
By grace alone, my heart does unfold,
The freedom from desires, a treasure to behold,
Transcending material lust, my soul is consoled.

Foolish was I, neglecting my true lover,
Within my heart, *Vishnu* doth hover,
The beloved of all beings, the soul's discover,
I'll forsake false identity, His embrace to cover.

Like *Lakshmi*, the Goddess, I'll seek delight,
In the soul's pleasure, shining so bright,
Content and faithful, in the Lord's sight,
My body, sustained by Providence's might.

No more seeking external desires in vain,
Inward with my eternal beloved, I'll remain,
The source of true love, my heart shall regain,
In the bliss of the soul, eternal happiness I'll attain.

* * *

    Pingala realized that the greatest happiness in the world was attaining eternal bliss at the lotus feet of Bhagavan Vishnu, and she had been wasting her life till now in the pursuit of carnal pleasures and lusty desires which would give her nothing but sorrow and misery. She decided to surrender herself to the Supreme Being hereafter with **Vairagyam** *(austere detachment). She realized that the soul in her body was the reflection of that Universal Spirit that is present in every living being and it is the only thing* that could give her eternal bliss and emancipation. "What is this body without a soul", she thought. "How could I forget the eternally blissful **Divine Spirit** that is situated in my heart! Hitherto, I had neglected Him and that was the cause of my distress. Unfortunately, I had been serving the bodies of ignorant men without realizing the real happiness lies elsewhere", lamented Pingala.

* * *

The greatest unhappiness arises out of **Material Desires** and **Lust for Carnal Pleasure**. Freedom from such desires gives rise to **Eternal Happiness** and bliss realized Datta. Carnal desires are the source of extreme sorrow in this world and **Desirelessness** is the source of perpetual happiness. This is achieved by surrendering at the lotus feet of **Bhagavan Vishnu**. This was the lesson he gathered from the story of the courtesan, Pingala.

Datta's observations - Summary

PINGALA

At Bhagavan's feet, eternal bliss is found,
Pingala once sought transient joy around,
In carnal pleasure, her life unwound,
Misery embraced her as sorrow crowned.

Neglecting the great Soul deep inside,
She sought delight in bodies that hide,
Her heart distressed, truth brushed aside,
Happiness within, she failed to confide.

But now she knows, the truth untold,
Real joy resides, within her soul's fold,
Embracing the bliss, her spirit extolled,
At Bhagavan's lotus feet, happiness she holds.

HAWK

Next morning, Datta woke up early and bid farewell to the old woman thanking her for her kindness in accommodating him for the night. She gave him directions to reach the temple and Datta went on his way. Soon he found himself in a large marketplace which was full of hawkers selling vegetables, fish, and meat. The din was deafening. Datta tried to avoid this crowd and sidled up the street towards the end of the market. As he walked along the street, he saw a hawker carry a basket of fish on his head, shouting to attract customers.

Suddenly a large hawk swooped down from the skies and made away with a large fish. Datta watched in fascination as the bird gracefully glided in the sky with the fish firmly held in its talons looking for a perch in the branches of a nearby tree to feast on its new catch. It alighted on the branch of a nearby tree and began pecking at the fish. Immediately, two or three other birds which appeared to be ravens attacked the hawk to relieve it of its morsel of food. The hawk took to the skies with the fish firmly clutched in its claws. But it was surrounded by two more hawks which began attacking it with their talons and pecking at it with their sharp beaks. The poor hawk tried its best to dodge the other birds but was injured by them. The hawk lost a couple of feathers in this conflict, and they floated to the ground. The hawk, finally tired of the attacking birds, let go off the fish that it was carrying. The other birds greedily swooped down to snatch the falling fish. The injured bird flew on to the branch of the tree to preen itself and nurse its injuries.

Watching this, Datta walked further on towards the temple which he saw at a distance thinking about the hawk and its meal. The poor bird had acquired a large fish from the market, but other birds did not allow it to enjoy its spoils. It was attacked by the other birds and ultimately, it found peace only when it let go off the fish.

* * *

Datta reflected that **Attachment creates Misery**. *As long as the bird was holding on tightly to its catch, it was heckled and attacked by other birds which were intent upon getting the fish for themselves. Often man running after worldly possessions and material pleasures encounters the same trouble from other individuals. Man is always craving for worldly possessions and intent on amassing wealth and material assets. On the other hand, others who are jealous and greedy are bent upon appropriating the wealth and possessions of his through hook or by crook. They may go to the extent of injuring others to acquire their property.* **Greed** *and* **Avarice** *often drives man to extreme* *wickedness that he does not hesitate even to murder his fellow men to seize the possessions of another.*

Amassing wealth and running after sensual pleasures in life often leads to misery and sorrow. This was brought out by the example of the hawk which had to let go off the fish that it had snatched for its meal. So also, unless man learns to let go off his possessions and attachments to the objects of the world, he would never experience peace in this world. The secret of survival in this world lies in abandoning the sensual pleasures in life. Learning the art of **Renunciation** *leads man to everlasting peace. This was the lesson Datta learnt from the hawk.*

* * *

Datta realized that **Attachment** brings on **Misery**. Man's attachment to worldly possessions often leads him to anguish and sorrow. The **Greed** and **Avarice** of fellow men causes agony for the man who runs after **Wealth**. **Detachment** ultimately gives lasting **Peace**. Datta realized this observing the episode of the hapless hawk. Datta smiled to himself when he realized the profound meaning in this simple episode of the hawk and the fish.

He walked on till he reached the temple and sat down on the *mandapam* outside the temple. The evening sun was casting long shadows and people were beginning to come to the temple for attending the evening Pooja and *Deeparadhana* (worship with the lamp) which took place at dusk.

Datta decided to go to the river near the temple and bathe before attending the *Pooja**. He would perform his *Sandhyavandanam* before reaching the temple. He would spend the night at the *mandapam* of the temple and partake of the *Prasadam* that the priest would give him after the *Pooja*.

Datta's observations - Summary

HAWK

In pursuit of wealth, man's desire soars,
As greed takes hold, their hearts implore,
They cling to treasures, material gain,
But others covet these, causing pain.

The bird that clutched its meat so tight,
Met torment from predators in flight,
Just like the human's worldly strife,
Engulfed in misery, forgetting life.

But wisdom speaks from nature's grace,
The lesson learned from bird's embrace,
To find true peace, one must release,
Attachments wane and joy increase.

In renunciation lies the key,
In happiness from wants set free,
The saintly know this truth profound,
In letting go, tranquility's found.

CHILD

Datta bathed in the cool waters of the river and sat on the banks of the river admiring the natural beauty all around. Birds were singing in the tree above him and a few bunnies and squirrels were scampering around. A few herons and egrets were wading in the shallow waters of the river trying to catch fish. A woman was washing clothes in the river and her child, a toddler, was playing on the banks of the river. The child was naked except for a G-string which covered his loins. Datta watched in fascination as the child, though alone, seemed to be extremely happy. At times he would chase a bunny which would scamper into the bushes. Occasionally, the child would enter the shallow waters of the river and splash about. At times he would try to catch a bird that alighted near him to peck at some worm on the grass. The child was laughing to himself all the time and running about in ecstasy. Datta remembered that his *Guru* had told him that a toddler would laugh daily at least three to four hundred times! No wonder, the child was elated and running about laughing all the while. Often, he would lose his balance and fall to the ground. But immediately, he would pick himself up and resume his play.

* * *

The innocent child is oblivious of the world and is content and involved in himself. He had no thoughts about a house or possessions. Honor and dishonor were unknown to him. Praise or insult, they never bothered him. The child was always happy enjoying his own company, reveling in himself. Children do not always need any companion to entertain them. They bear no grudge towards anybody nor are prejudiced or discriminatory towards others. They are free from anxiety for the future or regrets for the past. They live in the present. Anger, jealousy, greed, arrogance, and hatred are emotions that are alien to a child. The child is always happy with his life. He is least bothered where his next meal comes from, unlike the adult who is always anxious about the future. The child eats food only when he is hungry and does not eat a bit more than what he needs. He turns his face away when his mother tries to feed him, if he feels that he is satiated.

Datta reflected. A saint and a wise man are like the child. They exhibit the innocence of childhood. The child learning to walk falls many times, but never gives up. He immediately rises and tries to walk again. He always endeavors to continue what he is doing. Wise men too learn from their failures. They never brood over their shortcomings and lose heart but learn from their failures and move forward with renewed vigor. This is a lesson which is to be learnt from a child.

If a person stumbles on a stone on the road and falls, he curses the stone knowing fully well that it was his own carelessness which caused him to fall. But if a child falls, he does not blame the world, he just dusts himself, gets up and keeps on playing. Wise men should learn this trait from the little child. **Man thinks of his future when young and broods on the past when he is old**. This makes him sad his whole life. **Because happiness is an emotion that can exist only in the present**. A child is always happy. He lives in the present, neither depending on the past nor the future. Wise men and saints are like this.

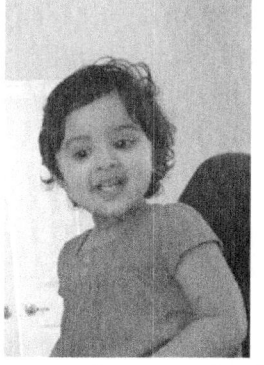

Even when a child falls and hurts himself and cries, it is only short-lived. Within no time he gets over it and resumes his efforts at play. He does not dwell moping on his fall. He knows that the pain has passed, and he should no longer hold on to it. The wise likewise learn to say, 'This too shall pass' and get on with life.

For the saintly person, his own soul is the source of entertainment for him. The saint and the wise like the child transcend the passions of the three Gunas – Sattva, Rajas and Tamas and exist in a higher plane always engrossed in the blissful thought of the Absolute Supreme Being or Brahman. But at the same time they function in the material world outside just like any other person diligently executing their duties towards their family and society.

A child never spends or wastes his Time in petty thoughts. He is always engaged. A child never sits idle. So also, the wise and the saintly do not fritter away their time in small talk or gossip but are always engaged in Karma doing their duty or meditating on the Brahman.

* * *

Datta was surprised by these thoughts that flashed through his mind giving him an insight into the innocence of childhood and how it taught him a very meaningful lesson. He shook his head in bewilderment. Strange are the ways of Providence, he thought. Even a simple toddler could instill in him such deep doctrines and profound spiritual truths! He wondered at the blessings of nature. The child taught him to find happiness not externally but within himself.

A child finds **Happiness** in **Solitude**. Neither **Regrets** of the past nor **Anxieties** of the future bother him. Saints also exhibit such an **Innocence** of childhood. Like a falling child lifts himself up, the **Wise** rise anew from **Failures** in life and go forward. **Happiness** is an emotion that can exist only in the present. A child never holds on to his **Pain** or **Sorrow** for long. He lets it pass and forgets it. So do the saintly and the wise.

Datta collected his things and walked towards the temple where he intended to stay for the night after the evening *Pooja* was over. Before he retired for the night, Datta resolved to make a note of his observations about the child he had observed that day.

Datta's observations - Summary
CHILD

In innocence, the child is pure delight,
Untroubled by praise or words that smite,
No grudge, nor hate, nor jealousy in sight,
Content with self, a beacon shining bright.

A saintly trait, this simple way,
To eat when hungry, no more they weigh,
No worry for the future's sway,
In present joy, their spirits play.

Like children pure, the saints aspire,
In the now, they find desire,
Bouncing back when they expire,
Failure's lessons, they acquire.

The past and future, not their care,
In present bliss, they freely share,
No idle thoughts, no time to spare,
In noble deeds, they find repair.

So let us learn from children's grace,
In every moment, find our place,
In innocence, we'll find our trace,
And saints and sages, we shall embrace.

MAIDEN

The next day morning, Datta left the temple after the morning *Pooja* and *darshan*. He decided to seek alms from any household he saw on the way. Datta had been away from his *Guru's Ashramam* for almost three months now and it was time that he returned. Hence, he decided to retrace his steps and move in a northerly direction aiming to reach the *Ashramam* within a few days. He trudged along the streets of the city and by noon was near the outskirts. He found a small single-storied house near the periphery of the city with a cowshed at the back and a small veranda in front. A large horse-drawn four-wheeled carriage stood in front of the house. A coachman stood nearby. There were guests in the house, presumed Datta. From the large, decorated coach and the coachman, Datta surmised that the visitors perhaps belonged to an affluent family. He decided to seek alms from the house and be on his way. He went to a side entrance of the house which was close to the dining area and called out,

"Amma, I am a sannyasi traveling north. Please give me some food."

The door was opened, and a beautiful maiden of sixteen or seventeen stood at the door. She was wearing a necklace of beads and on her wrists were many bracelets made of *Shanku* (conch shells). Young unmarried women wore conch-shell bracelets.

She gestured to Datta to wait and returned inside. She seemed to speak to someone who was in the main hall of the house. She returned to where Datta stood, and in a soft whisper said, "My parents are not at home. They have gone to the temple. There are a few guests at home who have come with a marriage proposal for me. Swamiji, there is very little *Rava* (semolina) in the home now. So, I have to pound some wheat quickly to prepare a little *Upma* (a cereal dish) for the guests. So, it will be a while before I can give you any food. Can you please wait in the lean-to here while I prepare the food? I will serve you as soon as I have pounded some wheat and cooked some *Upma*." So saying the maiden went inside.

She started pounding the wheat in a mortar using a long pestle. As she began doing this, the bracelets on her wrists made a loud jangling sound. The maiden muttered to herself, "Oh! hearing the noise of the bracelets, the guests will think that I am pounding wheat as there is no *Rava* in the house. They may have a low esteem about my family. I should reduce this jangling noise."

So saying, she removed all but two bracelets from each wrist and began pounding the rice again. Even the two bracelets in each wrist were still making a slight tingling noise. The maiden then removed one bracelet from each wrist and continued pounding the wheat. The single bracelet produced no sound. She completed the pounding and, in a jiffy, prepared some *Upma* and served her guests with a smile.

Soon, the parents of the girl arrived and engaged the guests in conversation. The maiden came outside with a plate of steaming *Upma* which she placed reverently in front of Datta along with a brass tumbler of water and stood nearby. "Swamiji, please have this humble food which I had to prepare in a hurry. I am sorry that I could not provide an elaborate meal for you", she said with concern in her voice.

Datta smiled, "Child, I saw your dilemma and was glad to see how you handled the situation efficiently and cleverly. May *Bhagavan* bless you with all prosperity and may you be blessed with a noble and befitting husband." He blessed her. The girl stood there with folded hands.

Datta finished his meal and, thanking the young maiden, began his trek towards the jungle which would take him north towards his father's *Ashramam*.

* * *

As he walked along, Datta contemplated on what he learnt from the episode of the nubile maiden and her bracelets. The loud jangling noise of the bracelets was reduced only when she removed all but two from each wrist. But still a tingling, disturbing noise remained. Hence, she removed one more pair of bracelets and continued her work silently with only one bracelet in each wrist.

When more than one person is present to work towards a goal, occasionally this could lead to chaos, arguments, and unnecessary discussion. Hence Datta felt that for proper spiritual advancement and practice, one should live alone and practice alone. Even when two persons lived together this could lead to discussion or worthless conversation which can affects one's spiritual aspirations. Hence to achieve the goals with single minded devotion and dedication, the wise men prefer to practice in solitude and not in groups. **Solitude was the companion of the saint**. This was a great lesson that Datta learnt from the episode of the maiden.

In our worldly life too, when too many people are involved with a project or working towards an objective, it may lead to chaos and quarrel and mar the progress towards their achievement. Hence the importance of limiting the number of persons involved in an important project or sensitive enterprise be it material or spiritual. This is an important lesson that is derived from this episode. Co-operation is essential, of course, for the successful completion of many projects. But one should realize that when **Concentration** and **Focus** are needed to complete a task, it is always better done is **Solitude** as against group endeavor.

When working as a group, conversation tends to dissipate into irrelevant gossip thereby deviating from the focus of the main theme. This can retard progress. Dissention and disagreement are wont to happen when a large number of people are involved in a venture. **There is always peace in solitude**. A student studying for his exams or a scientist working towards a momentous discovery would prefer solitude to a crowd. Contemplation and meditation are done in silent seclusion and not in a boisterous environment. This single minded devotion is what Datta came to understand from the maiden.

* * *

Datta remembered that the maiden removed all but one bangle in each wrist to avoid the jangle of the bangles. **Solitude** is best for **Spiritual Progress**. There was bliss in **Solitude**. A crowd generates irrelevant gossip. Even two is a crowd when **Contemplation** and **Concentration** are required in one's spiritual journey. Being **Reclusive** and spending time in **Quietude** are the attributes of saints and the wise.

Datta walked towards the jungle hoping to cross the jungle before sundown and reach the village which lay beyond it so that he could spend the night in the village. He hastened his pace.

Datta's observations - Summary

MAIDEN

In bangles' glimmer, chaos cries,
A noisy clatter, as they entwine,
Yet one alone in silence lies,
A solitary bangle, so divine.

A group of souls, a task they share,
Debate and discord, in their wake,
In solitude, the wise declare,
Spirituality finds its stake.

For focused study, silence calls,
In contemplation, wisdom thrives,
When conversation's noises enthralls,
Our goals, it often connives.

Cooperation's hand we need,
For worldly projects, vast and grand,
But in seclusion, hearts can heed,
The whispers of the soul's command.

The saintly souls, they comprehend,
The value of being all alone,
In solitude, their spirits mend,
To higher realms, they're gently flown.

So let us seek the quiet space,
Where meditation's light is sown,
In solitude, we find embrace,
And wisdom's seeds are fully grown.

FLETCHER

As Datta reached the outskirts of city where the jungle began, he heard a loud commotion at the end of the street and saw a large crowd coming towards him. There were mounted horsemen holding spears with swords hanging from the scabbards in their waist. In front of them were a band of drummers beating their drums to a rhythmic tune. Behind the horsemen was a caparisoned elephant with a *Howdah* (<u>decorated seat</u>) atop its back. The *howdah* had a silken canopy above decorated with frills. Sitting on the howdah was the king of *Videha*. He was returning after hunting in the jungle. The king wore a purple colored robe of silk and sported a single gold chain around his neck. His pleasing and benevolent attitude enraptured the crowds. He was waving to the crowd on either side of the street with a broad smile which indicated that he was genuinely pleased seeing his subjects.

People chorused his name and shouted his praise. Some showered flowers at the king. The people of *Videha* were ecstatic on seeing the king. Behind the king marched a retinue of his soldiers and on the rear were his minions carrying the hunted animals which consisted of deer, foxes, rabbits, and fowl. The cacophony produced by the procession and the drumbeats was deafening to the ears.

Datta stood mesmerized as he watched the king's retinue sluggishly move forward. The crowds surged around him and to avoid the congestion, Datta moved backwards and stepped into a shed on the side of the street. It was the shed of a fletcher. His arrow-making tools and equipment lay scattered in the shed. The fletcher himself was engrossed in making and sharpening an arrow and attaching fletching to the end of the arrow. He was engrossed in honing the tip of the arrow to a sharp point and concentrated his efforts on sharpening the arrowhead, frequently checking it to see if the shaft was perfectly straight and the tip was sharp. The fletcher was so absorbed in his job that he was oblivious of the royal extravaganza that was passing by his workshop. The noise of the kettledrums were deafening. Still the fletcher was undistracted and immersed in his work amidst the din and bustle of the cavalcade. Datta turned towards the fletcher with fascination amazed at his single-minded concentration.

This set Datta thinking. He understood that the fletcher, through his single mindedness conveyed a very important message. His unwavering focus on what he was doing gave Datta another item of knowledge to add to his repertoire.

* * *

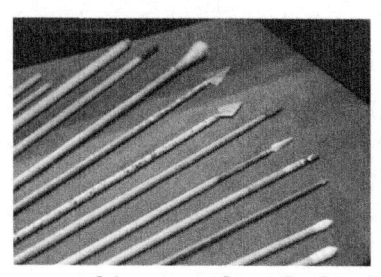

*To attain one's goal in life, the most important requisite is **Focus and Concentration**. The fletcher's focus on sharpening the arrow did not veer a bit even when the king's procession with all its din and bustle passed by him. A saint should realize that his practice of spirituality should also be focused and pointed like the fletcher. The mind should never waver from its goal. For a saintly person the goal is the realization of the Brahman and Moksha. To achieve this salvation, the sage should practice single-minded devotion towards God. One's spiritual advancement is often marred by the absence of focus and concentration in one's spiritual efforts.*

*Bhakti is the road to Mukti (<u>salvation</u>). To gain Mukti, one should totally surrender to God. For this it is not necessary to offer to God flowers or fruits, gold or jewels, lamps or aarti, sacred water or offerings. It is not the rituals or apparel of the devotee that matters. **Surrendering one's mind to God is Bhakti**. The greatest offering a person can give God is control of one's sense organs. Qualities like Compassion, Peace, Tapas, Shraddha*, Patience, and Truth should be developed in one's mind. This is the greatest offering one can make to God. These flowers of divine traits should be cultivated in the garden of our hearts and offered to God. **Bhakti calls for simplicity.** Ostentation, luxury, and grandeur are the destroyers of true bhakti. Many don't bother to understand this. Many do not realize that often false bhakti ends up seeking material benefits from God. That is why many fail in their spiritual journey towards Moksha.*

In the material world too, success is achieved only when one is wrapped up on the goal to be achieved and strives toward it with unwavering focus of the mind. In the third chapter 36th verse of Bhagavad Gita, Arjuna asks Sri Krishna, 'How can we control our minds?' Arjuna asks, 'Who makes me commit sins? I am not really intent on committing sins, I do not want to commit any sin. But I feel that some power influences me to commit sins. Which is that power which goads me to commit sins? Why does this happen? It repeatedly compels me to commit sins. What is that power?'

This was Arjuna's question. 'Why am I not able to understand this? Why do I waver from my goals in life? Why do I lose my focus and concentration? Why do I slip into committing sin naturally?' This is a question asked by everyone as to why one is unable to control his mind.

Sri Krishna answers, "Your knowledge is completely enveloped by a magical shroud. This is the eternal enemy of a knowledgeable person. This shroud called **'Kama'** *is a fire which cannot be quenched. Kama means "insatiable desire". It is that power which you cannot control, which turns into Kama. You can never satisfy it. The more you try to quench the fire of Kama the more vigorously that fire will burn. This is why the mind becomes restless. This is why the mind does not come under control. Hence, you are not able to concentrate on your goals. This is what makes you lose your focus. Kama distracts your mind away from your goals in life and may retard your progress towards success."*

This is true of the Brahmachari (<u>student</u>), Grihastha (<u>householder</u>), Vanaprastha (<u>retiree</u>) and the Sannyasi

(renunciate). *A student should be absorbed in his studies and concentrate on acquiring knowledge and experience during his student days. A householder should be focused on earning wealth through honest means for the upkeep of his family and caring for his parents and serving society. A retiree and a renunciate should spend his time focused on spirituality and attaining the true knowledge of the Brahman and spend his time immersed in religious pursuits. This is the only sure shot way in life to achieve success.*

* * *

This great truth dawned on Datta when he saw the fletcher working on his arrows undisturbed by the pageant that passed by. The fletcher exhibited **Focus** and **Concentration** in his work unruffled by the cacophony around him. The wise focus on their goals with **Single-minded Concentration**. The saint's focus is on attaining *Moksha* despite all the distractions around him. The shroud of *Kama* envelopes one's mind and detracts it from its goals. **Success** in life can be achieved only with **Focused Concentration** on one's goal. This was a great learning experience that Datta assimilated from the fletcher.

Datta's observations - Summary

FLETCHER

In life's pursuit, focus is the key,
Like fletcher, arrow-sharp, undistracted, and free.
With saintly grace, honing skills profound,
Concentrations dance, a rhythm unbound.

To *Moksha's* gate, surrender pure,
Not wealth, nor gold, but mind's allure.
The saints, the wise, their hearts aligned,
In *Bhagavan's* embrace, true peace, they find.

Kama's fire, deludes the mind,
Its unquenched flames, goals misaligned.
The wise, they see, and strive to tame,
To stay on course, in life's grand game.

Through every stage, duty's call,
A certain path, success enthralls.
The saints, the wise, in harmony they see,
Focus on purpose, the way to be.

SERPENT

The king's entourage had passed and the crowd in the street cleared. Datta continued his journey towards the edge of the jungle. The sun was descending into the horizon, and he had to cross the densest part of the jungle before sundown and find a suitable place to camp for the night. He decided to quicken his pace. As he walked along the beaten path which had been made by the previous travelers, he found dense bushes on either side of the pathway. Hearing a soft hissing sound, Datta paused to see what the noise was. In front of him he found a serpent slithering out of a hole in an empty termite mound. Datta remained quiet not wanting to disturb the slimy reptile. The snake came out of the hole silently and as Datta watched, it began rubbing its snout against a rock and continued doing so. Datta watched fascinated as gradually, its skin began to crack and Datta realized that the serpent was beginning to molt its skin. This process continued as the snake went on rubbing its body against the rock. Datta watched the serpent with fascination as it kept on molting its skin.

Datta decided to move on and cross the jungle and reach the other side. He moved quickly without disturbing the serpent.

Presently Datta came out of the jungle and reached the outskirts of the next village. He was happy to learn that he was nearer his *Ashramam* now. Near the village he found an abandoned temple. As the sun was descending towards the horizon, Datta decided to rest that night in the abandoned temple. He found a clearing around the temple and a well of clear water near it. A bullock cart was stationed nearby, and the two oxen were grazing tethered to the tree. Perhaps traveling tradesmen had stopped by for the night. There was a small *mandapam* at the entrance of the temple. Datta placed his bundle and his other possessions there. He went to the well and found a rope with an earthen vessel tied to it. Perhaps the travelers were drawing water from the well to quench their thirst, he thought. Datta drew some water from the well, drank the cool water and washed his face, hands, and feet. He returned to the *mandapam* planning to retire for the night. As he sat there, he began thinking of the serpent which he had seen in the jungle.

* * *

The serpent also had something to teach him. The snake was a lonely creature avoiding the company of other creatures in the jungle. It travelled alone not mingling with other snakes either. It moved silently and unobtrusively. A saintly person is also like that. He prefers the solitude in his spiritual journey and often avoids crowds in his travel. He is silent unless spoken to or requested to speak.

The serpent lives in dens and burrows made by other creatures like the vacant burrows of rodents, vacant termite mounds, or the hollows of trees. It does not have a home of its own, nor does it make a nest for itself. The saint is like that. He knows that a permanent home is the beginning of the life of attachment. A home will lead to a family – first a wife and then children finally leading to material possessions which have to be amassed for maintenance of the family. All these lead to attachment and goes against his goal of attaining liberation. Hence a sannyasi also, like the veritable serpent does not own a home, but moves from place to place making a home of convenience wherever he goes. He, like the serpent, prefers to live in the cave of his own heart without a pre-arranged abode.

He had seen the snake molting, and this gave him an insight into the human body. The human body is ephemeral. At the end of one's life, everyone has to discard the body which returns to the Panchabhootas whence it was created. The Soul, however, migrates to another body to start a new life. This is the **Law of Reincarnation** *which controls all living beings. the Karma that each one accumulates in one's lifetime decides the next incarnation. A saint aspires to break this cycle of birth and death or Samsara to reach the stage of eternal bliss where he merges with the Supreme Brahman never to be born again. Like the snake casting off its skin and assuming a new skin, the soul casts of this body to gain a new body, thought Datta. The verse from the Bhagavad Gita came to mind.*

वासांसि जीर्णानि यथा विहाय
नवानि गृह्णाति नरोऽपराणि ।
तथा शरीराणि विहाय जीर्णा-
न्यन्यानि संयाति नवानि देही ॥ २-२२॥

Vāsāṃsi jīrṇāni yathā vihāya
Navāni gṛhṇāti naro'parāṇi
Tathā śarīrāṇi vihāya jīrṇā-
Nyanyāni saṃyāti navāni dehī

Just as a man casts off his worn out clothes and puts on new ones, so also the embodied Self casts off its worn out bodies and enters others which are new.

* * *

Datta smiled to himself as the esoteric philosophy of the serpent's life stuck him. Like the serpent, **Silence** and **Solitude** are the hallmarks of the saint who prefers to live alone. The itinerant saint also, like the serpent, **Never Owns a Home** but prefers to occupy whichever place is available during his travels. It was the possession of a home that tended to induce **Attachment** in a saint and **Renunciation** was the only way to give up attachment. The molting snake made Datta realize the **Ephemeral Nature of the Human Body** which had to die and the soul **Reincarnate** in another body destined by his Karma. One's **Karma** during the present life determined the future reincarnation when one gives up this body and the soul gets into another body.

He pulled out the script from his bundle and with his stylus made notes about the serpent and its dwelling and its molting.

Datta's observations - Summary

SERPENT

In dens of rodents, serpents roam,
Among ants and hollowed wood they're known.
A saint, too, seeks a place not his own,
Prefers solitude, a life unshown.

A home, a family, breeding ties,
Attachments form, which often bind.
But saints, enlightened, truly wise,
Shun possessions, and free their mind.

Like molting snake sheds its old skin,
The soul leaves the body, starts anew.
Karma decides the form within,
A cycle, a journey to pursue.

Possessions fuel attachment's sway,
Deterring souls from their ascent.
The wise and saints know the way,
Detached from worldly entrapment.

In borrowed dens or lives serene,
Two tales converge, a truth profound.
Serpents' slither, saints unseen,
Lessons shared, in whispers found.

SPIDER

Datta ate the fruit that he had collected from the city and quenched his thirst with water from his *Kamandalu*. He decided to sleep on a raised podium on the *mandapam* and placed the bundle of clothes under his head as a pillow and lay down on the floor of the mandapam. It was a full moon night, and the moon shone in the east bright and large showering its silvery beams on the ground all around. Two travelers were in deep sleep at the far corner of the mandapam oblivious to Datta's presence. They had lit an oil lamp which cast its flickering light which shone on the roof of the *mandapam*.

Datta lay staring at the ceiling of the *mandapam*. There were sculptures of birds and animals on the roof faded with age covered with grime and moss. In the corner of the mandapam, hanging from a beam Datta spied a large spider. It was beginning to spin a web. The spider was dangling from the ceiling held by a thin silken thread and descended slowly as it extruded the thread from the glands in its abdomen. It was hanging by the thread and swinging from side to side trying to get a purchase on the side of the pillar which stood nearby. Every time the spider tried to hold on to the pillar, it missed and lost its grip. The spider continued swinging like a pendulum multiple times till it got a foothold on the pillar and gradually began the process of spinning its web. First it produced a few of radials. Then it fortified the center of its web with five or six circular threads. Then using its own body as a measuring device, the spider began spinning its spiral orb going around in circles from the center outwards completing a geometrically perfect spiral orb web. Finally, the spider migrated to the center of the web and waited patiently for its prey. It lay quietly at the center of the web as if meditating.

Datta watched captivated at the spider's perfect geometrical architecture. Strangely, the spider's web, though extremely sticky, did not ensnare the spider. Presently, a tiny moth fluttering nearby accidentally flew into the web and was snared in it. The spider briskly ran towards it and with a few strands of thread wrapped it into a bundle completely immobilizing it. Then it gradually fed on the insect biting into it. Datta watched the whole event spellbound as he drifted into a tranquil sleep.

The next morning Datta woke up early as he had to finish his journey that day. If he started early, he could reach his *Guru's Ashramam* before sunset. He went to the well nearby and drawing water from the well, bathed himself. The village was nearby, and he hoped that he would be able to gets alms from the village to appease his hunger. He drank a mouthful of cool water from the well and returned to the *mandapam* to collect his belongings.

Casually, Datta glanced up at the roof of the mandapam and was surprised to see the spider gradually eating its web. The web was shrinking in size. The previous day's moth which the spider had fed on, had shrunk into a tiny speck of dust. The spider was moving around the web ingesting it. He knew that spiders did eat and digest their web to produce a new web later on at a different place. He sat thinking of the previous days goings-on and remembered the spider spinning its web. His mind began ruminating on this thought.

* * *

Datta reminisced about the lessons that he learnt from the spider. Just as the spider creates and expands a web from within itself, the Supreme Consciousness or Godhead creates the whole universe with all the living and non-living creations from within Himself. He maintains it for millennia and at the end of a Kalpa (<u>4.32 billion years</u>) withdraws the whole universe unto Himself by annihilating it. This is called **Pralaya*** *(<u>dissolution</u>) which occurs at the end of every 1000 Chatur Yugas*. This is like the expansion of the web by the spider and its withdrawal of the web into itself by consuming it. The Supreme Godhead also functions like this in the universe. This expansion or creation of the universe and its withdrawal or dissolution is done without any external aid.*

During the whole process, the Godhead remains alone and unattached to the universe but functioning to create and maintain it with the help of Time. This is like the

spider which remains 'unattached' to its web even though it wanders all over the web. When the time comes, the retraction of the universe is done by virtue of the same power. The Supreme Godhead creates the five elements – Earth, Air, Space, Water and Fire and from them creates the universe incorporating the three **Gunas*** *– Sattva, Rajas, and Tamas. The sense perceptions of Touch, Taste, Smell, Vision, and Hearing are incorporated into these along with the* **Anthakaranam*** *which consist of the* **Manas** *(*mind*),* **Buddhi** *(*intellect*)* **Chittam** *(*memory*) and* **Ahamkaram** *(*ego*).* **[See Appendix at the end of the book]** *Thus is created Man, who is the highest form of living organism endowed with the power of logical thinking and reflecting. His ultimate goal in life is to realize this great truth and merge with the Godhead or Brahman. For this he has to undergo rigorous spiritual discipline to achieve Moksha (*salvation*).*

*All the creations in the universe ultimately rest in Him, the Godhead, like pearls and jewels in a string of necklace, where He forms the Sutra (*string*) that holds all these gems together.*

But the web that man weaves – the webs of intrigue and deception often entangles him and consumes him. We weave complicated webs of intrigue which often cause our own downfall or the downfall of others like the insects caught in the spider's web.

Another caveat, Datta reflected, that he gained from the spider was the **Quality of Persistence**. *Never give up was what the spider taught him. In spite of failing many times initially, the spider had persisted in its efforts and finally succeeded in constructing its web against many odds.*

If you use an axe to chop down a tree, the tree may fall after a 100 chops. One does not believe that the 100th cut would have been enough. The other 99 chops were not a waste. No, because the 100 cuts were needed to make the tree fall. Each cut contributed to the fall of the tree. But one achieved the result only after the 100th attempt. A person's efforts in life are also like this. If one keeps on trying and does not get any result, he may be frustrated. One should not forget that the all efforts will bear fruit. Sometimes, one may give up his efforts before he reaches the final result. If the person with the axe stopped after the 99th cut, he would not have felled the tree. So one should not rest till he completes the task and gets the result. If he puts in effort he will definitely get a result. Man's resolve is so powerful.

Some persons live always cursing their life, without reaching anywhere. They often start new ventures in life but abandon them halfway. They are unable to complete what they started, their attempts fail, and they withdraw dejectedly from what they started. This is what is called 'failure'. But there is another circumstance in many an individual's life which is more dangerous than this. These individuals do not even begin or attempt anything worthwhile in their life. This is worse than starting a venture and then failing halfway through. Not having the grit to start anything is the worst type of failure. These individuals fear failure halfway through their venture and hence never attempt to begin anything worthwhile. Even before starting they think of failure and do not start any new venture in their lives. Hence their sorrows are also unfounded. So, before starting a new venture in life, one should not be too anxious about it. Even if one starts and fails, that is an experience for him. He learns from it. One *always learns from one's failures. So, when one begins afresh, he will have this additional experience taught by his failure and it will help him overcome any difficulties that he would face. But if he does not start at all thinking of failure, he is sitting on the peak of foolishness.*

Just as the spider expands its web, the **Brahman** creates the **Universe** from within Himself. At the end of a **Kalpa**, like the spider, He withdraws it unto Himself. The Brahman remains **Unattached** to the Universe like the spider and its web. The quality of **Persistence** was another trait Datta learnt from the spider by observing its numerous attempts to spin its web. **Perseverance** in the face of **Failure** was another precept he imbibed from the spider. **The failure of the mind is the greatest failure, and the victory of the mind is the greatest victory**. This was the greatest lesson that Datta learnt from the spider.

* * *

Datta sat on the raised platform of the mandapam munching on some fruit. He had to leave shortly as he had to cover a considerable distance before he would finally reach the *Ashram* of his *Guru* and father, sage *Atri*. As he looked up at a pillar at the corner of the mandapam, he saw a wasp busy building its nest with mud brought from outside. He sat there and watched spellbound by the architectural prowess of the wasp. Datta decided to record his musings about the spider and its web lest he forget the details. Datta smiled to himself as he took out his palm leaf script to record his musings. He would begin the final leg of his journey towards his home once he made a note of the information.

Datta's observations - Summary

SPIDER

In the realm of nature's artistry,
A spider weaves its tapestry,
From depths within, threads interlace,
A complicated web takes shape.

As does the Supreme Godhead wise,
Creating realms beneath the skies,
The Universe with cosmic thread,
To which all lives and worlds are wed.

Within the heart of mortal clay,
Five elements in fusion play,
Anthakaranam's subtle chord,
In man's creation, all afford.

Yet, man with webs of intrigue weaves,
Entangling hearts with sly deceives,
Downfall awaits those who conspire,
To fan the flames of wrongful fire.

From spider's craft, let's learn the art,
Of diligence, a vital part,
To persevere, despite the plight,
And weave success through darkest night.

Fear not to venture, heart be bold,
For those who risk, a tale unfolds,
Failures may come, but wisdom's found,
In learning from each hallowed ground.

So like the spider, spin with zeal,
In life's grand tapestry, reveal,
Rhyme your journey, stanza by stanza,
In this grand cosmic opera.

WASP

The wasp flew in with a tiny ball of mud held between its front legs and alighted on a corner of the roof adjoining a pillar. It pressed the ball of mud into a corner of the roof and smoothed it with its head. All the time it was making a high-pitched humming sound as it worked. It fashioned a small, elongated tube of mud after a few excursions, each time bringing a small blob of mud. The wasp designed its nest with the dexterity of a potter.

Datta continued his breakfast of fruit and water as he watched the wasp's nest. Promptly the wasp returned with a small caterpillar and stuffed it into the long tubular nest. It sat on the mouth of this tube making a continuous buzzing sound for a long time.

Datta had seen such mud dauber wasps in his home in the woodwork and in the walls in his garden. The wasp would continue to return to the nest all the while buzzing and humming loudly. Ultimately, over a few days, the caterpillar would get transformed into a wasp and emerge from the nest as a full-fledged wasp.

Legend is that the caterpillar, which is inside the nest, hearing the continuous loud humming from the wasp is scared. It constantly keeps thinking of the wasp and ultimately gets metamorphosed itself into a wasp. This legend set Datta thinking. [*For the true scientific explanation, see Annexure*]

*   *   *

When the mind is focused constantly on a thing, be it out of love, fear, or hatred, it tends to becomes transformed into that object. When one's mind is always fixed on an object or thought, it tends to change one's character. Whatever a man thinks constantly, he becomes. A person always contemplating on evil ways tends to become a personification of evil and wickedness. A person who constantly harbors good thoughts in his mind like kindness, sympathy, love, compassion etc., tends to develop these qualities and change his character and behaviour.

यद् भावं तद् भवति - Yad Bhavam, Tad Bhavathi.

You become what you think

A person who contemplates constantly on the Absolute Godhead ultimately reaches Him, Datta reflected. When a person habitually thinks of the spiritual and philosophical eminence of his Guru, he too tends to become a spiritual master like his Guru. A seeker unceasingly meditating upon God tends himself to become divine.

The story of the sage Bharatha from the Srimad Bhagavatham endorses this. The sage Bharata was a king who had given up his throne and accepted Vanaprastha (living in the forest). One day he chanced to see a lion chasing a pregnant doe. The doe jumped into the river to escape from the lion but could not cross the river and in panic died giving birth to a little fawn. Sage Bharatha saw the fawn get *carried away by the river and rescued the little deer and brought it up to his Ashramam and fondly looked after it. The sage got so much attached to the little deer, that he was continually thinking of it and even in his deathbed, his thoughts centered around the deer. Ultimately, when he died he was re-born as a deer in his next incarnation. This story dawned on Datta as he thought of the wasp and the caterpillar.*

When a man constantly meditates on the Godhead and spends his time surrendering all his activities to Him, he ultimately attains Moksha and merges with the Supreme Being. This is what Datta realized from the incident of the wasp and the caterpillar. This was why saints and wise men unceasingly contemplated on the Bhagavan and always spent their time listening to His praise, His stories, and His songs. Taking part in Satsangs and conducting Satsangs, they spent their time continually in the thoughts of the Supreme Brahman in order to attain salvation.

A mind constantly thinking of positive thoughts always leads the person to success. Endless negativity plaguing one's mind tends to lead one towards failure and sorrow. Thinking incessantly of success always makes success an attainable goal. Failure, on the other hand engulfs one who is constantly chiding and criticizing fate for his downfall. A person who carries thoughts of joy and happiness in his mind always tends to be happy whereas the gloomy one constantly brooding on his fate and ill-luck is always given to sorrow and depression. This is the lesson that one learns from the wasp and the caterpillar.

* * *

Just as the caterpillar constantly thinking of the wasp becomes transformed into one, the saint who constantly contemplates on the **Brahman** attains **Moksha** and merges with Him. A mind centered on **Positive thoughts** meets with **Success** and **Happiness** in life. **Negativity** of mind paves the way to **Depression, Sorrow,** and **Failure**. A **Sattvic Personality** is the result of **Pleasant** and **Cheerful thoughts** whereas **Evil Thoughts** assailing the mind lead to a **Malicious Personality**. This, concluded Datta, was what he learnt from the wasp.

Smiling to himself, Datta got up from where he sat and gathered his belongings. It was time to begin the last lap of his journey which would get him back to where he started from – his *Ashramam*. With a light heart, happy at what all he had achieved during his adventures, Datta began walking towards his Ashramam where his father and Guru sage Atri and his mother Anasuya awaited him with eager expectation. He was sure that if he quickened his pace, he could be home by sundown. Happy with himself, and single minded resolve, Datta began the last leg of his trek towards his home.

Datta's observations - Summary

WASP

In fear, the caterpillar's thoughts doth flow,
Of wasp's sharp sting, it trembles in woe.
Through transformation's grace, it doth transcend,
To be the wasp, its fear doth mend.

Man's mind a canvas, thoughts do paint,
Constant musings determine his fate.
Positive hues, a happy song they sing,
With success and joy, their wings take wing.

Yet negative shades, a sorrowful dance,
Lead to failure's realm, no second chance.
Contemplation divine, on *Brahman's* shore,
Leads to *Moksha's* embrace, forevermore.

Worldly objects allure, a binding spell,
Like Bharatha and deer, a tale to tell.
Evil thoughts in constant stream,
Shape a wicked soul, a darkening dream.

But *Saatvic* thoughts, with saintly art,
Illuminate the path to the divine heart.
The wise doth know this timeless law,
As a man thinketh, so shall he draw.

In thoughts we weave our destiny's thread,
Be mindful, dear soul, of what lies ahead.
For within the minds eternal flight,
A man becomes the essence of his light.

EPILOGUE (MY BODY)

Datta prostrated before his father and *Guru*, sage *Atri*. He had taken four months and seven days to complete his practical education in the lap of *Nature* and had returned to the *Ashramam* a changed man. The sage Atri held him by the shoulders and bade him stand up.

"Sit down", the sage told him pointing to a mat on the floor beside him. "How was your journey? What did you learn from your exploits?"

Datta folded his hands and replied, "I learnt much more from my travels than from the scriptures you taught me. My lessons were derived from the practical experiences that I went through and the observations that I made as you had advised me. I applied the six **Pramanas** which you had advised me about and analyzed every bit of information asking the questions of **Why, How, What, When, Where** and **Who.** I encountered twenty-four eminent *Gurus* during my travel who taught me all that I know. That has made me into what I am today. My outlook on life has totally changed and I have learnt the art of '***Detached Concern***' with the world and with all that is in it."

"That is wonderful", commented the sage, "tell me all about your twenty-four *Gurus*".

For the next hour, Datta recounted the knowledge and wisdom that he had gained during his travels occasionally referring to his palm leaf manuscript and concluded with the episode of the wasp and the caterpillar. He read out to his *Guru* the verses that he had composed regarding the twenty-four *Gurus*.

The sage smiled in satisfaction. "Well done, my boy," he said, "Your education is now three-fourth over. You can move into the world to gain the rest of the knowledge in the years ahead. I am sure that you are now qualified to accept the life of a *Grihastha*.*"

Datta bowed his head and said, "After learning from the twenty-four *Gurus*, I realized at the end that the greatest *Guru* of all is my own body which taught me more than everything put together."

Sage Atri raised his eyebrows. "How is that?"

"I shall briefly explain what I learnt from my own body after I went through my experiences with the twenty-four *Gurus*." So saying, Datta explained what he learnt from his own body.

* * *

Our own body is to be considered as a superior Guru as it teaches us many truths. The body is born, grows and undergoes death and decay. But in the process, it helps us gain a lot of knowledge and acquire wisdom. To learn the philosophical principles with our Anthakaranam*, we need a body. But we know very well that the ultimate fate of the body is death and decay. The body is the device that makes this learning possible. This thought helps us detach ourselves from the body emotionally and focus our thoughts on the Supreme Godhead that made all this possible. Thus, the body itself teaches us **Detachment**.

The body also gives us the knowledge about **Discrimination** and **Discretion** due to the presence of Ahamkaram within us. This is lacking in the bodies of other living beings like plants and animals. **Our greatest Guru is our own Atman** (soul). One must realize this truth. If we do not have the inclination, no one can teach us. But only if we have the right mindset and the predilection, can we understand these great spiritual truths.

If man gets too much attached to the body, he proceeds to earn wealth to maintain it. Then he expands his needs for a wife, children, house, cattle, and such material possessions. The continuous efforts to amass wealth and possessions leads to sorrow, and spending this wealth on his family and others leads to frustration. There is no end to **Kama** (intense desire) which is like the sacrificial fire. The more ghee you pour into it, the more the fire blazes forth. You can never douse a fire with oil. Thus trying to satisfy the needs of his own body and that of others, man's life comes to an end.

The human body is like a house, the Soul its owner and the senses are like his many wives. Satisfying each sense like the **sense of sight, hearing, touch, taste, smell,** and the **sexual desire** is like satisfying the needs and wishes of many wives. The person is thus torn among his various 'wives' and loses his mental balance and peace. That is what always trying to satisfy one's senses does to an individual. Hence, one should not give in to the **Temptations of One's Senses** but should endeavor to keep them under control.

The human body is a gift of God and so we must respect it. It is an inevitable medium needed for man to realize the Supreme Godhead or Brahman. This can be realized with one's Anthakaranam and unless the human body is healthy, this will not be possible. Hence, it is our duty to nurture the body and keep it healthy and fit. The other creatures like animals, birds or reptiles too are endowed with a body and the senses, but they do not have the capacity to realize the truth about the Brahman using their body. This is because of the absence of Anthakaranam in them. **Man is the only creation that can realize the Supreme Godhead.** Hence the saints and the wise men take care to **Nourish the Body** with the minimal amount of food needed to keep it healthy, active, and fit. The Yogic practices are directed to this end.

The Jeevatma (Soul) attains a human body after undergoing numerous cycles of birth and death. Hence man should strive to use the available life to **Realize the Truth about the Godhead** and reach the ultimate perfection of life as long as his body is healthy and functioning.

The human body is the only equipment that we have in this world to make us understand these spiritual truths and philosophical principles. We should accept a spiritual teacher or Guru in life to learn these. But many a time, one spiritual mentor may not be sufficient to learn all that is to learn in spirituality. Hence there is no harm in resorting to study from different spiritual masters.

Man seeks knowledge to Develop the Perfection in himself. Both material knowledge and spiritual knowledge are within him. But as it is enveloped by a shroud of ignorance, it is not obvious to him. Acquiring knowledge is the process of removing that envelope of ignorance. How do we remove it? Sparks fly out of a rock only when it is subject to friction using another rock. Similarly, to generate the spark of knowledge in an individual, a great Guru is needed. Only a Guru can remove the ignorance and promote knowledge in a person. A Guru does not give birth to the disciple, but the Guru teaches him to face life by helping him develop various skills. A man should search for an appropriate Guru early in life. But unfortunately, many get this inspiration to seek a Guru only after a major part of their life is over. It is like searching for a guide when our journey is almost over. **We need a Guru at the beginning of the journey of life, not at the end.** Those who do not think of this necessity get stuck halfway through. Their life may end in tears. This is the sad truth about life.

It is known and affirmed that the Soul in every living being in the universe is part of the Supreme Godhead or Brahman. This is an irrefutable conclusion. Hence learning from the various other life forms and creations in the world is also part of our spiritual education. To this end, the moth, the serpent, the wasp, the pigeon, and a legion of living forms teach us lessons in spirituality and wisdom. Some such beings give **Positive Instructions** like the python, the bumblebee, the hawk, the child, and the serpent which teach us what is the good thing to do. Whereas other creatures like the elephant, deer, fish, pigeon, and the moth teach us what **Not** to do. These **Negative Instructions** are as important as the positive ones. Hence, understand that the **Soul** in all creatures on earth including man reflects the Supreme Godhead and we should imbibe the knowledge and wisdom imparted by them. Both the positive and negative instructions enrich our spiritual knowledge. We should understand the **Unity in all living beings despite their Morphological Diversities**.

We have to understand that in this world, the best friend we have is **Ourselves**. You are your own best friend. Ask yourself questions when you are in doubt. Ask yourself how you would solve a problem; ask yourself how you would like to be happy and contented. The answers will surprise you. **Answers to all questions are within you. Solutions to all problems are also within you.** Look into the mirror to recognize the friend in you. For the mirror reflects not only your body, but your soul too. Look inwards to gain the true knowledge.

There is nothing that **Man's Strength** cannot subdue. The truth is that man does not use his strength in the right manner, in the right place for the right reasons. Man can conquer the skies, the oceans, and the earth. Man has been able to control even the strongest animals on earth. Man has converted metals into weapons. But why is he not able to solve even the small problems that he faces in daily life?

The reason is that man approaches problems **Emotionally**. An emotional approach will weaken an individual. If emotions cloud one's attempt to solve a problem, then the power of discrimination will be clouded by them. **Emotions** and **Discretion** are two states of the human mind. In some circumstances, one has to function emotionally but in others discretion is required. But if one uses emotional solutions to solve a problem where discretion and discrimination are called for he may fail because emotions may not offer the solutions. Emotions do not arise from one's intellect. Emotions arise out of one's circumstances, one's body's state and one's mindset. But **Discretion** and **Prudence** arise out of a person's wisdom. **Emotions are whisperings of one's 'heart' whereas Discretion is the briefings of one's 'head'.**

Hence, there is nothing that one cannot achieve in the world. But if one approaches a problem emotionally, he will become weak and encounter failure. But if he uses **Discretion** and **Discrimination**, success will be his to achieve. Hence in all circumstances of life instead of emotion, discretion and discrimination should be put to use in approaching problems. But to acquire the power of *discrimination, one must acquire adequate knowledge and wisdom. If one fails to do so, he may face failure in all aspects of life. Because* **Knowledge** *and* **Wisdom** *are the weapons that lead one from failure to victory.*

A mother has to undergo labor pains to deliver a child. After nine months of agony carrying the child in the womb, she has to undergo severe labor pains during delivery of the baby. It may be a second life for the mother. But look at either ends of this pain. The happiness of a marital life is the beginning and the happiness of having the child is the end. In between the mother undergoes endless woes while pregnant and during childbirth. Thus, **alternating Pain and Enjoyment is the Law of Nature.**

Thus, if one has to undergo pain or suffering in life, he will encounter happiness and joy at the end of the pain. One should always compare his suffering with the joy that he would have experienced previously. So, in life pain and suffering are inevitable. If one enjoys happiness, he should be ready to suffer pain also. There cannot be monsoon without summer. A pleasant spring always follows a harsh winter. So are the pain and suffering in life. One should not be disheartened by the sufferings in life. Always feel that there is hope of happiness after the suffering like light at the end of the tunnel. Thus, one should always live life with the hope of joy and happiness after sorrow or pain.

* * *

Datta's observations - Summary

MY BODY

In the house of flesh and bone,
The Soul resides, the senses prone,
Desires drive, man's heart does race,
Control thyself for lasting grace.

A gift from God, this body divine,
To seek the truth, the soul align,
Nurture health for the spirit's flight,
In paths of the Supreme, take flight.

Ignorance veils man's inner light,
A *Guru's* wisdom clears the night,
Within us dwells the Supreme Soul,
All life forms part of the grand whole.

Our greatest friend, we are to be,
Seek answers deep, set questions free,
Look inwards for the knowledge vast,
Solutions lie within the heart's vast.

Emotions sway, the heart's delight,
Discriminate with the intellect's might,
Decisions wise, let reason steer,
And let not passions interfere.

Life's tapestry weaves pain and pleasure,
A mother's labor, a joyous treasure,

Sorrow's cloak, joy follows near,
In cycles, life's dance does appear.

In verses woven, wisdom shines,
Through rhymes and rhythm, truth aligns,
Within these stanzas, truths unfold,
In each line, life's lessons told.

* * *

"After all my wanderings learning from *Nature*, ultimately, I came to realize that the greatest *Guru* was my own body and the *Atman* that lies within. I had wandered in search of Knowledge and Wisdom around the world little realizing that the greatest teacher was within me. Now I realize that **My Body is the greatest Guru** that teaches me everything that I have to know."

Datta completed his long explanation and looked expectantly at his *Guru* with folded hands and bowed head.

"You have achieved the greatest knowledge that anyone can acquire", said the Guru. "You can begin sharing your knowledge with others and teach disciples henceforth."

"I have one humble request", said Datta. "After my realization of the truth and my education, I have come to realize that I should be dedicating my life to the realization of the *Brahman* and am planning to spend my life as an *Avadhoot*. I do not entertain thoughts of a householder's life and hence please forgive me and bless me to lead the life of a sannyasi. I am not interested in getting shackled to a *Grihastha's* life."

Sage Atri was taken aback. He was expecting his son to assume the responsibilities of a *Grihastha* on return from his pilgrimage. But here the boy was yearning to become an *Avadhoot* – *a person who has passed beyond all worldly attachments and concerns*. His two other sons were well into spirituality but married. Datta was aspiring for a life of spirituality renouncing all worldly pleasures and concerns. But sage Atri, who was a *Sthithaprajna* (of balanced mind) quickly recovered himself and smiled at Datta. "So be it," he blessed Datta laying his hand on his head.

Datta once again prostrated before the sage and severing all ties with his family and the world, walked out into the dusk. Sage Atri sat there staring at the receding figure of his son silhouetted against the setting sun. He was now an *Avadhoot* and detached from the material world forever.

The sun set in the horizon, but the full moon rose shining from the eastern horizon to bring on another night of silvery brightness. **'Every end heralds a new beginning'**, thought sage Atri.

ANNEXURE

Advaita : Advaita means "non-secondness". It indicates that *Brahman* alone is real and the undivided Supreme Consciousness and all individual souls (*Atman*) are part of the *Brahman*. It is a monistic theory. The soul (*Atman*) in each living being is the same as the Universal Soul (*Brahman*).

Agasthya [story] : Sage Agasthya was one of the famous sages in Hindu Mythology. He is one of the seven Rishis (*Saptharishis*). He figures in the *Ramayana* and the *Mahabharata*. There is a story about him and the two Rakshasa brothers.

According to Valmiki's Ramayana, there once lived two Rakshasa brothers, Vatapi, and Ilvala. All their life they killed holy men by tricking them. Vatapi had the boon of transforming into any life form at will. While Ilvala had the power to bring back the dead.

In order to kill the sages, Vatapi would take the form of a goat. Ilvala would assume the form of a holy man. Every time sages passed through the forest, Ilvala would invite them for a feast. Ilvala would then kill and cook the goat, which was Vatapi, and serve it to the holy men. After they were done feasting, Ilvala would shout, " O Vatapi! Come out." Vatapi would emerge tearing the stomach of the sages. The rakshasa brothers thus killed thousands of holy men using this ruse. One fine day, Ilvala saw Sage Agasthya passing by. As usual, he invited the sage for a feast. Sage Agasthya, through his divine powers, understood that he was being tricked by the Rakshasa brothers. However, he decided to play along. As expected, Ilvala cooked the goat and served it to Agasthya. After the feast, Ilvala shouted "O! Vatapi, Come back". But Sage Agastya after eating the meal, rubbed his hand over his belly and said, "Vatapi has been digested." Thus Agasthya put an end to the Rakshasa Vatapi. Ilvala fell at the feet of Agasthya and sought his forgiveness and mended his ways thereafter.

Anthakaranam : The human brain has four levels of function. Together, these are called the 'Anthakaranam'. They four levels are the *Manas* (mind) which receives the sensory perceptions, *Ahamkaram* (Ego) which gives us our self-esteem and self-importance, *Buddhi* (Intelligence or Memory) which is the human ability to discriminate and rationalize and

Chittam (Intellect) which is the ability of reasoning and logical understanding.

Ashram -Ashramam : Both mean the same. It is a spiritual hermitage or a Hindu monastery where saints and sages live. In ancient times, it was the place where scriptures were taught by the *Guru* to the *Sishyas* (disciples) who stayed in the *Ashram*. This is called the *Gurukulam* system of education – a residential teaching institution.

Ashtanga Yoga : Yoga constitutes a group of physical, mental, and spiritual practices to discipline the mind and the body to ultimately unite with the Brahman. *Ashtanga* (eight limbs) *Yoga* was advocated by sage Patanjali. It is the eight-fold path of Yoga. The eight 'limbs' are : *Yama* (abstinence), *Niyama* (observances), *Asana* (posture), *Pranayama* (control of breath), *Pratyahara* (withdrawal of senses), *Dharana* (concentration), *Dhyana* (meditation) and *Samadhi* (Trance).

Avadhoota : A person who has reached a stage of spiritual development in which he is beyond worldly concerns ; A Renunciate

Avatar : The incarnation of a deity in human or animal form to counteract and destroy evil in the world. Usually the Avatars of *Bhagavan Vishnu* are referred to as the '*Dasavataram*' (ten avatars).

Brahma Muhurtam : It means "time of Brahma" and indicates the predawn period when one's mental faculties are at its best. It is the best time of the day to indulge in spiritual practice and study. The Brahma Muhurtam corresponds to two muhurtas before sunrise (1 muhurtam = 48 minutes). Hence it is 1 hr. and 36 min before sunrise. (4.30 am to 6 am if the sun rises at 6 am).

Brahmachari : The true meaning of *Brahmachari* is 'one who follows the path of Brahma'. It is usually equated with the student life of an individual. Cleanliness, *Ahimsa* (non-violence), simple living, studies, meditation, and voluntary restraints or abstinence are the characteristics of a *Brahmachari*.

Brahman : *Brahman* is the concept in Hinduism which denotes the unchanging Reality. It is the omnipotent, omniscient, and omnipresent entity which is equated with the Supreme Godhead which is the source of all creation. All souls of living beings are part of the *Brahman*.

Brahmana : *Brahmanas* are the priestly class or the teachers according to the Varna Ashrama in Hindu society. [see the section on **Varna**]. It has to be distinguished from the *Brahman*.

Chatur Yuga : *Yugas* are 'eons'. There are four *Yugas* which come as a cycle. The first is *Krita Yuga* (1,728,000 years), the second is *Tretha Yuga* (1,296,000 years), the third is *Dvapara Yuga* (864,000 years) and the fourth is the *Kali Yuga* (432,000 years). The present one is *Kali Yuga*. One cycle of four such *Yugas* is called *Chatur Yuga*. One thousand such *Chatur Yugas* constitute one *Kalpa*.

Dharma : The literal meaning of Dharma is 'that which supports'. It has been variously translated as 'duty', 'righteousness', 'merit', 'conduct' and 'religious duty'. It is the moral code for living. It also means the inherent nature of a thing e.g. the nature of fire is to burn.

Dvandvas : It means a pair of opposites like pain and pleasure, good and evil, joy and sorrow etc.

Dvija : Literally means 'twice born'. Brahmin, Kshatriya, and Vaisya boys are initiated into spiritual studies after the 'Upanayanam' ceremony between the ages of 7 and 13. This is considered their 'second birth'.

Ganga : The river Ganges in India is held sacred by Hindus. The goddess of the river is named Ganga.

Gayatri Mantra : This is a mantra in Rig Veda which was composed by the sage Vishwamitra. It is chanted to achieve success and happiness in life. It is directed toward the sun (*Savitur*) which is considered the manifestation of *Brahman*.

Grihastha : There are four stages of life of a person according to Hinduism. They are *Brahmachari* (Student), *Grihastha* (householder), *Vanaprastha* (retiree) and the *Sannyasi* (renunciate). These are called the four *Ashramas* (stages) in a Hindu's life.

Gunas : They mean 'attribute' or 'property'. There are three Gunas namely, *Sattva* (goodness ; calmness), *Rajas* (passion ; activity) and *Tamas* (ignorance ; laziness). All three are present in all things – animate and inanimate – things in the world. The proportion of these may differ giving different characteristics to the individual.

Guru : A *Guru* is a personal spiritual teacher. He acts as a mentor, guide, and counselor for the disciple or *Sishya*.

Gurukulam : The Gurukulam system of education in ancient India was a residential system where the disciple lived with the Guru and his family in his *Ashramam* and learnt the scriptures, various spiritual truths, and practical skills from the teacher. The usual period of education was for 12 years but was variable depending on the aptitude of the student.

Hatha Yoga : It is the branch of Yoga that deals with the development of the body by means of exercises (asanas) and *Pranayama* (control of breath).

Japa : It is the repetition of a mantra or a divine name. *Japa* is mostly done along with meditation. It is also used to mean chanting the various names of the deities. E.g. *Vishnu Sahasranamam, Hanuman Chalisa, Venkatesa Suprabhatham.*

Jatharagni : It refers to the 'digestive fire' present in the stomach and duodenum which digests food. This is a term used in Ayurveda to denote the 'inner fire' in the abdomen which is needed for metabolizing the food.

Kalpa : [See *Chatur Yuga*] Four *Chatur Yugas* forms one *Kalpa*. One *Kalpa* is one day (12 hours) for *Bhagavan Brahma* (4.32 billion human years)

Karma : Literal meaning of *Karma* is 'action'. It is used in Hinduism to explain the universal principle of cause and effect. Good *Karmas* yield positive results and bad *Karmas* negative results. The *Karmas* (actions) of a person in this life is carried over to the next incarnation and the sufferings and joys of the present life are due to our *Karmas* in our past lives.

Kubja : When Sri Krishna visited the kingdom of Kamsa for the first time as a teenager, prior to killing the wicked Kamsa, he met a hunchbacked woman in the market place. Her name was Kubja. Out of pity for her, he removed her hunchback by pulling her up with his hands and his touch transformed her into a beautiful maiden.

Moksha : Liberation from the cycle of birth and death (*Samsara*) is called *Moksha*. The soul keeps on reincarnating in various bodies as it works its way up spiritually. Ultimately, the soul merges with the Supreme Soul or *Brahman* never to take birth again. This is *Moksha*. It is also called *Kaivalyam*.

Mrithyunjaya mantra : It is a mantra from Rig Veda directed to Shiva. It is believed to ward off premature death, calamities and bestow longevity.

Narada : Sage Narada is a divine sage, the son of Brahma, one of the Trinity. An ardent devotee of *Bhagavan Vishnu*, he travels around the worlds singing the praise of the *Bhagavan*. He acts as a messenger for the Gods and his interventions often produce salutary results.

Neem tree : This is the Margosa tree and has an important role in Hinduism. It has medicinal properties and is revered as the abode of gods.

Pooja : Pooja is a method of worship of a deity with flowers, lamp, offerings etc. It is way of offering our homage to the deity. Pooja is also offered to inanimate objects like rivers, seas, mountains and trees.

Pralaya : The literal meaning is 'dissolution' or 'annihilation'. At the end of one Kalpa which is 4.32 billion years, all creation is believed to "dissolve" back into the *Brahman* from whence it came. This is called Pralaya.

Pramana : *Pramana* means 'proof' or 'means of knowledge'. It is the core concept of Hindu philosophy and the basis of all learning. There are six main *Pramanas* which help one to acquire knowledge. They are the logical ways to learn anything.

Prana : It means 'breath' or 'life-force'. Five divisions of Prana are described namely, *Prana Vayu, Apana Vayu, Samana Vayu, Udana Vayu,* and *Vyana Vayu*. These five Vayus govern different areas of the body and different physical and subtle activities.

Pranayama : Control of Breathing. This is a practice in Yoga where the inhalation and exhalation of air is controlled leading to calming one's mind. It has three steps Poorakam (inhalation), Kumbhakam (retention) and Rechakam (exhalation) and is done slowly. Inhalation is done through one nostril and exhalation through the other.

Prarabdha Karma : The Karmas performed by a person in previous lives are "carried over" to the present life which he is living as *Prarabdha Karma*. It is the "Fate" which we are experiencing now. The Prarabdha Karma cannot be changed as it is the result of our past Karmas.

Purana : The *Puranas* are ancient literature which were written centuries ago. They comprise the legend of Gods, their history, their powers, and parables connected with them. These stories are rife with the philosophies and doctrines advocated in the *Vedas* in a subtle form for the common folk to understand. There are 18 major *Puranas* and 18 minor ones.

Rakshasa : They are evil demons described in Hindu mythology. They can change their form at will as animals or monsters. They are cannibals and live in forests.

Rishyasringa [story] : Rishyasringa was a Brahmachari sage, the son of sage Vibhandaka. He was born with the horns of a deer. The sage Vibhandaka had brought up the lad in isolation in the forest away from the eyes of everyone. Hence the boy had not seen any woman in his life. He had followed the strict life of a Brahmachari ascetic and had magical powers owing to his strict spiritual practices.

Meanwhile, the kingdom of Anga ruled by King Romapada, was facing a severe drought. The sages opined this as to be due to curse of Indra, the God of Rains. The royal sages advised the king that the only way the country could survive this disaster was by bringing a chaste Brahmachari into the kingdom. They told him about Rishyasringa who had been brought up without setting eyes on a female at all.

The king Romapada sent a retinue of courtesans disguised as young Brahmacharis to the Ashram of Vibhandaka when the sage had gone to the nearby kingdom. They approached the ashram in a large boat disguised as a hermitage. They began singing songs sitting in their boat. The sweet melody wafted in the wind to reach the ears of Rishyasringa. He was captivated by their music and was drawn to these 'young Brahmacharis' who looked divine and charming and fell for them. He sat in their ashram in the boat and without his knowledge, the courtesans rowed the boat towards the kingdom of Romapada. As soon as the boat docked in the king's palace, it began to rain, and the king was overjoyed.

Later when Vibhandaka returned, he found his son missing and through his clairvoyant mind, he understood what had happened. In fury, he reached the kingdom of Romapada, but the king mollified him and gave his daughter in marriage to Rishyasringa thereby appeasing the sage Vibhandaka.

It was Rishyasringa who conducted the yajna for the birth of sons for king Dasaratha in the *Ramayana*.

Saatvic : Having Sattva *Guna* predominantly. Such persons have a mode of goodness in them. It is the *Guna* of positivity, calmness, purity, virtue, balance of mind, knowledge, and goodness.

Sanctum sanctorum : The sanctum sanctorum or *Garbhagriha* is the centermost part of a temple where the idol of the deity is placed. The rest of the temple is built around the *Garbhagriha* in the form of concentric circles or squares. Pooja is offered to the deity by the priest in the Sanctum sanctorum.

Sari : A garment consisting of a length of cotton draped around the body by women in India.

Shraddha : It is any act performed with sincerity and absolute Faith. It indicates single-minded concentration on a subject or object. It also means 'confidence' or 'intense devotion'.

Shruthi : Shruthi means 'that which is heard' and represents the *Vedas*. They were revealed or heard by the ancient Rishis during meditation. They are considered Divine revelations.

Sthithaprajna : It means 'firm in judgement and wisdom' or 'of balanced mind'. It refers to a man of steady wisdom.

Sudra : The Sudras form the fourth rank in the Varna or Caste system. The other three are the Brahmanas, Kshatriyas and Vaisyas. This Varna system was based on the character and occupation (*Guna* and *Karma*) as is explained by Bhagavan Sri Krishna in the Bhagavad Gita chapter 4 verse 13. [See **Varna**]

Upanayanam : The Upanayanam is a ceremony performed for boys between the ages of 7 and 13. They are given to wear the 'sacred thread' or *Yagnopaveetham* or *Poonal*. It marks the entry of the boy into his second birth, the stage of a Brahmachari when he is initiated into the scriptures.

Upanishad : The *Upanishads* are philosophical texts which were appended to the *Vedas* later and hence are also called *Vedanta* (end of the *Vedas*). They are in the form of a dialogue between the *Guru* and *Sishya*.

Varna : Society was divided into four classes -Brahmanas (Priests: Teachers), Kshatriyas (Kings : Warriors), Vaisyas (Traders) and Sudras (labor class) based on their **Occupation** and **Quality** and not on their birth. This is called the *Varna Ashrama*.

Veda : The *Vedas* are *Shruthis* which were divine revelations to the sages of yore. They were transmitted by word of mouth from generation to generation. These are considered Eternal Truths which are unchangeable.

Vedanga : Ancillary supportive texts to the Vedas are called Vedangas (limbs of the Vedas). There are six Vedangas for each Veda namely, *Siksha, Vyakarana, Chhandas, Niruktha, Jyothisha* and *Kalpa*.

Wasp : The wasp referred to in the book is the Mud Dauber Wasp. The wasp builds a nest using mud which it brings in small quantities. It builds a tubular nest and lays its eggs in it. The wasp catches spiders which it paralyses with its sting and stores them in the nest along with its eggs. When the eggs hatch into larvae (caterpillar), they feed on the paralyzed spiders. The larvae develop into pupae which mature into adult wasps and leave the nests. This is the life cycle of the mud dauber wasp.

The reference in the scripture to the caterpillar becoming the wasp is really the larva of the wasp maturing into an adult.

Yadu-Avadhoota Samvadam : This is the dialogue which occurred between King Yadu and an Avadhoota who was really sage Dattatreya. Here Dattatreya describes the 24 Gurus in Nature from whom he learned whatever he knew and contributed to his spiritual knowledge. This is the theme of this book.

RESOURCES & REFERENCES

1. **24 Gurus from Srimad Bhagavatham – Omkar Sharma**
   https://www.speakingtree.in/blog/twenty-four-gurus-from-the-srimad-bhagavatam
2. **How to Learn Wisdom from Nature – What Srimad Bhagavatam says about the Avadhuta who had 24 gurus. - C. V. Rajan.**
   https://hinduismwayoflife.com/2018/02/07/how-to-learn-wisdom-from-nature-what-srimad-bhagavatam-says-about-the-avadhuta-who-had-24-gurus/
3. **24 Gurus – Sree Datta Vaibhavam.**
   https://www.sreedattavaibhavam.org/24-gurus/
4. **Lord Dattatreya and His 24 Gurus**
   http://muneshkumarkella.blogspot.com/2013/05/lord-dattatreya-and-his-24-gurus.html
5. **24 Gurus of Nature   You Tube**
   https://www.youtube.com/watch?v=RUEmUqUurcI
6. **24 Gurus of Lord Shree Dattatreya**
   http://dandvat.com/twenty-four-gurus-of-lord-shree-dattatreya-avadhoot-prabhu-%E2%80%AA%E2%80%8Edandvatpranam%E2%80%AC/
7. **Avanti Brahmin's 24 Gurus**
   http://jagadanandadas.blogspot.com/2008/08/avanti-brahmins-24-gurus.html
8. **Story of Prostitute Pingala**

https://www.radhanathswami.net/yearwise/1991/91-110-story-of-prostitute-pingala-sb-11-08-22-27-by-hh-radhanath-swami-in-mumbai-2
9. **24 Gurus of Dattatreya – Nature if the greatest teacher.** https://sivanandayogafarm.org/blog/24-gurus-of-dattatreya-nature-is-the-greatest-teacher/
10. **Your 24 Gurus - Sri Srimad Bhakti Vedanta Narayana Maharaja** https://www.purebhakti.com/teachers/bhakti-discourses/24-discourses-2005/462-your-twenty-four-gurus
11. **24 Gurus of Dattatreya – Nature is the Ultimate Teacher.** https://vedicfeed.com/gurus-of-dattatreya/
12. **24 Gurus of Dattatreya – Nature is the greatest teacher.** https://debaratideb.medium.com/24-gurus-of-dattatreya-nature-is-the-greatest-teacher-f810adca9465
13. **8 lessons to learn from Nature.** https://www.intelligentchange.com/blogs/read/8-lessons-to-learn-from-nature
14. **5 Life lessons we can all learn from Nature** https://blog.tentree.com/5-life-lessons-we-can-all-learn-from-nature/
15. **Lessons we can learn from Nature In these times of climate change – Danielle Levy. (medium)** https://medium.com/@daniellelevynutrition/lessons-we-can-learn-from-nature-in-these-times-of-climate-change-ff730b3cd098
16. **What can we learn from Nature - Make me better.** https://www.makemebetter.net/what-can-we-learn-from-nature/
17. **20 Amazing life lessons Nature has taught us. - Marin Resnick** https://www.lifehack.org/articles/communication/20-amazing-life-lessons-nature-has-taught.html
18. **What does nature teach us? 14 lessons from the natural world -** https://nature-mentor.com/nature-lessons/
19. **Nature : 26 powerful lessons to learn from nature. – Tejal Patel.** https://www.purposefairy.com/68155/lessons-to-learn-nature/

20. 10 life lessons you can learn from observing nature - Pearl Nash.
    https://hackspirit.com/life-lessons-from-observing-nature/
21. 7 things to learn from nature - spiritual lessons from nature - The Spiritual Indian.
    https://www.thespiritualindian.com/things-to-learn-from-nature/
22. 24 Gurus of Dattatreya - Advaita-Vedanta - Samaneri Jayasara YouTube
    https://www.youtube.com/watch?v=ydKIx3Ky4K8
23. Wisdom from 24 Gurus You tube
    https://www.youtube.com/watch?v=7wvUmaHzqyM
24. 24 gurus of Avadhoot brahmana Part 1 HH Bhakti Rasamrita Swami You Tube
    https://www.youtube.com/watch?v=NZsDy7lWWJg
25. 24 gurus of Avadhoot brahmana Part 2 HH Bhakti Rasamrita Swami You Tube
    https://www.youtube.com/watch?v=SxNIsZiEf3s
26. 24 gurus in nature - Project Shivoham You Tube

    https://www.youtube.com/watch?v=d3FmsvxttNI&t=4s

27. Pramanas – A Vedic Learning Process for this Digital Age - Project Shivoham - You Tube.
    https://www.youtube.com/watch?v=PDQZ9C7yuDg
28. The history of Panchatantra - Project Shivoham - You Tube
    https://www.youtube.com/watch?v=_8zGxvOT6oQ
29. How we learn and grow. – Practical Sanskrit
    https://blog.practicalsanskrit.com/2009/12/how-we-learn-and-grow.html
30. Dattatreya - Wikipedia.
    https://en.wikipedia.org/wiki/Dattatreya#:~:text=He%20is%20described%20in%20the,to%20lead%20a%20monastic%20life.
31. Pramana - Wikipedia.
    https://en.wikipedia.org/wiki/Pramana
32. Pramana – Encyclopedia Britannica
    https://www.britannica.com/topic/pramana
33. Atri - Wikipedia
    https://en.wikipedia.org/wiki/Atri

BOOKS IN ENGLISH

1. Road To Success – Napoleon Hill -A Tarcher Perigee book 2016.
2. Making Habits, Breaking Habits – Jeremy Dean - Da Capo press 2013.
3. Atomic Habits – James Clear –
4. Sanatana Dharma – An Elementary Textbook of Hindu Religion & Ethics. Published by the Board of Trustees Central Hindu College, Benares 1916
5. Chariot of the Gods by Eric von Daniken, Berkley books, New York. 1999.
6. The Holy Geeta by Swami Chinmayananda. Publishers- Central Chinmaya Mission Trust, Bombay.
7. The Complete Works of Swami Vivekananda Published by Swami Bodhasarananda 17th Edition. Advaita Ashrama Publications. 1986. (9 Volumes – in English)
8. Bhagavad Gita by Swami Ranganathananda. (3 Volumes). Advaita Ashrama Publications. 1st Ed. 2000.
9. Brahma Sutras. -According to Sri Sankara by Swami Vireswarananda. Advaita Ashrama Publications. 12th Reprint 2014.
10. Srimad Bhagavatam. Eleventh Canto Parts 1 & 2. AC Bhaktivedanta Swami Prabhupada. 1984 Reprint 2021. The Bhaktivedanta Book Trust.

BOOKS IN MALAYALAM

11. Srimad Bhagavatham by Pandit P. Gopalan Nair. Guruvayur Devaswom Publications. 2017. (8 volumes – in Malayalam).
12. Ganesh Puranam by Thottayil N. Krishnan Nair -Vidyarambam Publications. 1st Ed. 2003.
13. Sri Siva Maha Puranam by Swami Dharmananda Theertha. Kurukshetra Prakasan Publications. 3rd Ed. 2001.
14. Mahabharatam by V Ramakumar. Siso Publications. 12th Ed. 2009.
15. Sampoorna Ramayanam by Dr. P.S. Nair. Vidyarambham Publishers. 16th Ed. 2017.

16. Skanda Puranam by Thottayil N. Krishnan Nair – Vidyarambham Publishers. 3rd Ed. 1998.
17. Garuda Puranam by K. Kunhukrishna Pillai. Vidyarambham Publications. 7th Ed. 2004.
18. Srimad Bhagavad Gita Bhashyam – Sri Sankaracharya Virachidam by K. P. Ramunni Menon. Guruvayur Devaswom Publications. 2nd Ed. 2015.
19. Maha Bhagavatham by Dr. P. S. Nair. Vidyarambham Publications. 13th Ed. 2003.
20. Vishnu Puranam by K. Krishnan Kutty. Published by Devi Book Stall 1st Ed. 2003.
21. Srimad Bhagavad Gita by Swami Prakasananda. Published by Sri Ramakrishna Math. 1 Ed. 1967.
22. Manu Smriti by Swami Siddhinathananda. Published by Sri Ramakrishna Math. 1st Ed. (third reprint) 2016.

A Humble Request to the Reader

Thank you for buying and reading this book. May I request your indulgence for one more favor.

I hope you enjoyed reading this book and derived advantage from the *Story of the Avadhoota*.

Kindly give your sincere and valuable review of this book in the Amazon site. Your rating and candid review will be a great inspiration and encouragement to me.

I would also request you to check my other books – ***Tell Me a Story, Grandpa*** and ***Grandpa Tell Me More Stories*** which are a compilation of short stories with morals, written with children in mind.

Also, the book of '*In Search of a Bridegroom*' is an interesting Autobiographical Fiction which will be of great interest to the reader.

Two books on the Health Problems faced by the Elderly are available under the names, "***How to face the Health Challenges While getting Old***" and "***Old Age Health – Challenges and Solutions***" These deal with the Health Challenges in old age, their Early Recognition, Prevention and Treatment.

Understanding the Electrocardio- gram is my recent medical book written for the benefit of the Medical fraternity. It is a book for doctors, residents, and nurses.

The book *"**Demystifying Hinduism**"* is a book describing the Basics of Hinduism in a simple manner and is Book 1 of the series '*Understanding Hinduism*'.

ABOUT THE AUTHOR

Sahasranam Kalpathy (Dr. K. V. Sahasranam) is the author of seven books previously on various subject like Short stories for children, an Autobiographical fiction, a book on ECG and two books on Health Problems in Old age.

His books of Short Stories with morals, for children are named '**Tell Me A Story, Grandpa**' and '**Grandpa, Tell Me More Stories.**' His third book '**In Search of a Bridegroom**' is an Autobiographical fiction based on his first-hand experiences. He has authored two books in a series dealing with the Health Problems of Elderly persons namely '**How to face the Health Challenges While Growing Old**' and '**Old Age Health – Challenges and Solutions.**' His book on '**Understanding the Electrocardiogram**' is a handbook for doctors, medical residents, and nurses. His recent book is '**Demystifying Hinduism**' which describes the Basics of Hinduism in a Q & A format.

He is a retired Cardiologist settled in the U.S.

BOOKS BY THE AUTHOR

NON-FICTION

How to Face the Challenges while Growing Old
Problems of Elderly Book 1

Old Age Health Challenges and Solutions
Problems of Elderly Book 2

Understanding the Electrocardiogram
Medical Book on ECG

Demystifying Hinduism   Understanding Hinduism Book 1

The Avadhoota   Understanding Hinduism Book 2

Daily Musings   Understanding Hinduism Book 3

How to Master Essential Life Skills   Skill sets for Success Book 1

How to Achieve Professional Excellence   Skill sets for Success Book 2

FICTION

Tell Me a Story, Grandpa   Short Stories for Children Book 1

Grandpa, Tell me More Stories   Short Stories for Children Book 2

In Search of a Bridegroom   An Autobiographical Fiction

The Truth Lies Out There   A Family Drama of Suspense

Code Black   A Hospital based Thriller

Diabetes Demystified   Everyday Health Guide Book 1

Printed in Great Britain
by Amazon